W9-AFU-921

WITHDRAWN

WOMEN in MEDICINE

Elisabeth Kübler-Ross

Encountering Death and Dying

LOS ALAMOS COUNTY LIBRARY
Mesa Public Library
2400 Central Avenue
Los Alamos, NM 87544-4014

JB
K951W

Women in Medicine

Karen Horney
Pioneer of Feminine Psychology

Mathilde Krim and the Story of AIDS

Elisabeth Kübler-Ross
Encountering Death and Dying

Rita Levi-Montalcini
Nobel Prize Winner

Mary Eliza Mahoney
and the Legacy of African-American Nurses

Margaret Sanger
Rebel for Women's Rights

WOMEN in MEDICINE

Elisabeth Kübler-Ross

Encountering Death and Dying

Richard Worth

CHELSEA HOUSE
PUBLISHERS
A Haights Cross Communications Company
Philadelphia

COVER: Elisabeth Kübler-Ross at her farm in Virginia.

CHELSEA HOUSE PUBLISHERS
VP, NEW PRODUCT DEVELOPMENT Sally Cheney
DIRECTOR OF PRODUCTION Kim Shinners
CREATIVE MANAGER Takeshi Takahashi
MANUFACTURING MANAGER Diann Grasse

Staff for ELISABETH KÜBLER-ROSS
EXECUTIVE EDITOR Lee M. Marcott
PHOTO EDITOR Sarah Bloom
PRODUCTION EDITOR Noelle Nardone
SERIES & COVER DESIGNER Takeshi Takahashi
LAYOUT 21st Century Publishing and Communications, Inc.

©2005 by Chelsea House Publishers,
a subsidiary of Haights Cross Communications.
All rights reserved. Printed and bound in the United States of America.

A Haights Cross Communications ◀ Company

http://www.chelseahouse.com

First Printing

9 8 7 6 5 4 3 2 1

Library of Congress Cataloging-in-Publication Data

Worth, Richard.
    Elisabeth Kübler-Ross : encountering death and dying/Richard Worth.
        p. cm.—(Women in medicine)
Includes bibliographical references and index.
    ISBN 0-7910-8027-7
    1. Kübler-Ross, Elisabeth. 2. Psychiatrists—United States—Biography.
3. Death—Psychological aspects. I. Title. II. Series.
RC339.52.K83W67 2004
616.89'0092—dc22

                                                            2004009325

All links and web addresses were checked and verified to be correct at
the time of publication. Because of the dynamic nature of the web,
some addresses and links may have changed since publication and may
no longer be valid.

Table of Contents

Dr. Kübler-Ross, Death, and Dying

1

Down the long, spacious corridor of a major American hospital strode a small, dark-haired, Swiss-born psychiatrist. Dr. Elisabeth Kübler-Ross walked briskly toward the room of a patient who was dying of cancer. More than any other physician, Kübler-Ross had brought the subject of thanatology—the study of death and dying—out of the darkness and into the light of medical science. Most doctors were unwilling to talk to terminally ill patients about death. In modern medicine, which prided itself on curing patients, doctors regarded an illness that could not be cured as a sign of failure. Kübler-Ross realized, however, that the patients themselves wanted to discuss their terminal illness, and, as a well-trained psychiatrist, she listened.

One young man named Larry, for example, could not admit to himself that he had developed a terminal illness. He was a big man, accustomed to being in control of his life, especially his strong, young body. With Kübler-Ross's help, however, he began to come to terms with the disease that was rapidly killing him.

Other patients became angry that they had been singled out to be stricken by a terminal illness. They looked around them and saw so many other people enjoying their lives. "Why me?" they asked themselves. One patient told Kübler-Ross that he had become very angry at finding out that he had a terminal illness and had only a short time to live. As she told him: "Most of my patients react the same way. They are shocked and they are angry that their future has been taken away, but gradually they realize that they are still living today, that they still have a tomorrow. Because they have limited time to live, very often they live with more intensity and with different values, and enjoy life more, because they do not always plan for tomorrow and next year, the way healthy people do." [1]

Other patients try to postpone death as long as possible by bargaining with God or with their own doctors. One terminally ill woman asked Kübler-Ross if she could spend a day out of the hospital to attend her son's wedding. Then she would agree to lie quietly, take all her medicine, and accept the fact that her illness would probably end her life shortly. Kübler-Ross agreed, and the woman attended her son's wedding. However, when she came back to the hospital, she said to Kübler-Ross, "Don't forget ... I have another son." She was still bargaining and hoping to postpone death as long as possible.

As Kübler-Ross discovered, patients quite commonly had these reactions to their own terminal illness. In addition, people had similar responses—denial, anger, and bargaining—when their own child or another member of their family was dying. A common reaction was profound sadness. One woman wrote a poem, which she gave to Kübler-Ross about the coming death of her son:

> I saw a boy on a bike go by
> He was ten years old and blue of eye.
> Slender like you with straight blond hair
> But hard as I looked, you were not there.
>
> A group of children playing ball
> Boys and girls, both big and small.
> I was restless inside and the panic grew,
> Because try as I might, I could not see you.

Eventually, this mother achieved a sense of peace when she accepted the fact that her son was going to die. Some people, Kübler-Ross discovered, reached acceptance regarding their own death or the death of a loved one. Often this acceptance occurred as they talked with family and friends about death, sharing all their feelings. This woman's poem continued:

> I glanced up at the clouds as they billowed by
> Floating free in a peaceful sky
> Lovely and light—they have not a care
> And finally my son, I found you there.[2]

From her own experiences with death as a child, her volunteer work in Europe after World War II, her empathy for the sick and dying, as well as her training as a psychiatrist, Elisabeth Kübler-Ross revolutionized the field of terminal illness. Her work changed modern medicine, vastly improving care for dying patients across the world.

Early Years 2

The birth of Elisabeth Kübler, on July 8, 1926, was an unusual event, not only for her parents, but for the entire of city of Zurich, Switzerland, where she was born. After having a son several years earlier, Emma and Ernst Kübler, her parents, had longed for a daughter. However, they were very concerned by the baby they saw. Elisabeth was a tiny infant, only about two pounds, and her parents were afraid that she might not survive. They had little time to worry about this problem, however, because a few moments after Elisabeth was born, Emma Kübler gave birth to another baby girl, whom she named Erika. This was Elisabeth's identical twin. A few seconds later, however, a third little girl, Emma (later called by her nickname, Eva), was born. Instead of one daughter, the Küblers had triplets. Across Zurich, the Kübler triplets became instantly famous. They even appeared on billboards, advertising a popular brand of soap and a well-known chocolate drink.

While the triplets were still young, Mr. Kübler moved his entire family to the nearby Swiss countryside. The attic of the Kübler's new house became the triplets' playroom. Here they spent many hours enjoying their large dollhouse or putting on Mrs. Kübler's old clothes and playing dress-up. Holidays were particularly happy times for the family. On *Rabenliechtli*, similar to Halloween, the girls put on masks. Later in the year, they were visited by Santa Claus, who brought a large bag of nuts and candy and rewarded children who had behaved themselves and minded their parents. Finally, in the spring the Kübler children marched in the parades at *Sechselauten* and watched as a snowman made of cotton was burned to symbolize the passing of winter.

As the children grew, many people had trouble telling them apart. They looked the same, and Mrs. Kübler dressed them identically. Although the girls had no trouble getting along with each other, life as a triplet created problems for Elisabeth. "For me, being a triplet was a nightmare," she later wrote. "I would not wish it on my worst enemy. I had no identity apart from my sisters. We looked alike. We received the same presents.... On walks in the park, passersby asked which one was which. Sometimes my mother admitted even she did not know."[3] She also realized that each of her parents had a favorite. Her father favored Erika, and her mother favored Eva. Neither favored Elisabeth.

As Elisabeth grew, however, she found ways to distinguish herself from Eva and her identical twin, Erika. When Elisabeth was about five years old, she became fascinated with a picture book about Africa. A short time later, hearing that a troupe of Africans were performing in Zurich, she managed to sneak aboard a train and attend the performance. Eventually, she returned home to her frightened parents, who were convinced that something terrible had happened to her. Then Elisabeth proudly announced that she wanted them to give her a black, African doll.

When she was a child, Elisabeth's father called her his *Meisli*, which means "Little Sparrow"—because she was always so busy. One day he took her with him to watch horse racing, and they spent the entire day at the racetrack. Unfortunately, afterward Elisabeth caught a bad cold, which gradually turned into pneumonia. She was rushed to the hospital, and the harsh treatment she received there became one of the most memorable experiences of her early life. "The examining room was cold. No one said a word to me. Not 'Hello.' Not 'How are you?' Nothing. A doctor yanked the cozy blankets off my shivering body and quickly undressed me. He asked my mother to leave the room. Then I was weighed, poked, prodded, asked to cough, and treated like a thing rather than a little girl as they sought the cause of my problems."[4]

Elisabeth was moved to a bed alongside another little girl who was dying. It was Elisabeth's first exposure to death. However, even in the midst of her suffering, the girl tried to cheer up Elisabeth. "'It's important that you keep fighting,' she explained. 'You're going to make it. You're going to return home with your family.' … 'What about you?' I asked."[5] The little girl knew that she was dying, but she did not seem to be afraid. By the next morning, she had gone. Elisabeth gradually recovered, helped by a blood transfusion (a transfer of blood) from her father. Then, as she was about to go home, he brought her a surprise: a beautiful black doll.

Because of his financial success as the manager of a large office supply firm in Zurich, Mr. Kübler was able to move his family into an even larger home in the countryside. Elisabeth enjoyed playing in the woods and taking hikes with her father in the Swiss mountains. Roped together, they climbed over high cliffs and across massive glaciers. Once, Elisabeth fell through a hole in the rocks and might have been killed as the rope that held her started to rip. Mr. Kübler lowered another rope to Elisabeth, however, and pulled her up to safety.

During her walks in the woods, Elisabeth found wounded birds and built a small animal hospital inside her house to nurse them back to health. Mr. Kübler called her a *Pestalozzi,* after a Swiss hero who had helped the poor. One of her pets was a monkey named Chiquito, who had come from Africa. One day she took Chiquito to the local bakery. He became frightened by the other people in the shop and jumped off Elisabeth's shoulder, upsetting many of the pastries in the bakery window. Elisabeth was afraid that the bakery owner would tell her father, who might punish her. She discovered later, however, that news of Chiquito's antics had spread throughout the area, bringing more customers to the bakery than ever before. The owner was delighted.

THE COMING OF WORLD WAR II

As Elisabeth grew older, more challenges lay ahead for her. Shortly after her thirteenth birthday, Europe was engulfed in a terrible war. On September 1, 1939, German armed forces, directed by Nazi dictator Adolf Hitler, invaded Poland. The Polish army was no match for the powerful Nazi tanks and planes, which rapidly overran the country. Elisabeth listened to reports of the war on the radio in her parents' living room. As she heard about the courageous battle waged by the Poles, Elisabeth made a quiet promise to those people: "'I vow that unless I die, and no matter what else happens, I will come to your help as soon as I can.'"[6]

Elisabeth had no idea how she might fulfill this promise, nor did she expect that it might be done soon. Meanwhile, during the following year, the Nazis overran most of Western Europe. Switzerland did not participate in the war, but remained neutral. Nevertheless, Elisabeth's father and her brother joined the volunteers to patrol the Swiss border. They tried to help refugees who were fleeing the Nazis to find safety in Switzerland.

Blackie

Unfortunately, Mr. Kübler did not share Elisabeth's love of small animals. Among her pets was a group of rabbits that she had raised. Mr. Kübler, who enjoyed rabbit stew, directed Elisabeth to take one of these rabbits after another to the local butcher to be killed. During the 1930s, a Swiss father's word was law in his household, so Elisabeth did as she was told, no matter how much it hurt her. Finally, she had only one rabbit remaining, Blackie, whom she brought to the butcher to suffer the same fate as the others. That evening at dinner, Mr. Kübler tried to persuade his daughter to eat some of the tasty rabbit stew, like the rest of the family. But Elisabeth stoutly refused. "I reasoned that they obviously did not love me," she recalled, "and so I had to learn to be tough. Tougher than anyone. As my father complimented my mother on the delicious meal, I told myself, 'If you can make it through this, then you can make it through anything in life.'"*

* Elisabeth Kübler-Ross, *The Wheel of Life: A Memoir of Living and Dying*, New York: Scribner, 1997, pp. 37–38.

As the war continued, Elisabeth reached an important milestone in her life. Her interest in Africa and in healing sick animals had grown by her teenage years into exciting career plans. Elisabeth dreamed of three different types of careers— becoming an explorer in Africa, becoming a nurse, and her most cherished dream, becoming a doctor. By the age of 16, young people in Switzerland were required to decide whether they were going to pursue job training or apply for the gymnasium (junior college) and later a university education. One night after the girls had finished dinner, Mr. Kübler announced that he had decided what would be best for all three of them. Eva, he said, would go to a girl's school, where she would learn all the necessary skills to become a wife and homemaker. Erika, a very good student, was selected by Mr. Kübler to go to the gymnasium and the university. Finally, it was Elisabeth's turn. She hoped to follow the same path as Erika. Mr. Kübler announced that Elisabeth would instead follow in his footsteps, however, and enter the office supply business with him.

Elisabeth was stunned. She had absolutely no interest in going into her father's business. To the surprise of everyone at the table, she refused to do what her father wanted. "I'd rather be a domestic servant than join your business," she yelled.[7] No one was supposed to question Mr. Kübler, least of all his three daughters. He was shocked. Mr. Kübler told Elisabeth that as far as he was concerned, she could begin looking for a job and leave the house as soon as she found one.

With the help of her mother, Elisabeth obtained a position with a family in the western part of Switzerland, at Romilly on Lake Geneva. However, the duties she was expected to carry out almost overwhelmed her. Elisabeth was given a tiny room and expected to work 18 hours a day, with only one-half day off each week. Her employer, Madame Perret, constantly criticized her work, demanding that she do more and more cleaning and cooking. Meanwhile, Elisabeth almost collapsed from lack of food, because Madame Perret only allowed her to eat leftovers from the family meals.

At Christmastime, Madame Perret ordered Elisabeth to help prepare a large dinner party for a houseful of guests. Elisabeth was not permitted to enjoy any of the food herself, however. This last act of unkindness finally convinced Elisabeth that she must leave the Perret family. Packing a suitcase, Elisabeth tiptoed downstairs in the middle of the night. She borrowed a sled from the Perrets and rode across the snow to the train station. Then she bought a ticket, with the little money she had managed to save from her small wages, and headed home.

Elisabeth's father had not softened his position regarding her future. Since she still refused to enter the supply business, Elisabeth was ordered to find a job doing something else. Based on her interest in medicine and science, she decided to apply for a position working in a chemical laboratory. Her first job was short-lived, because the lab soon closed. She was successful in obtaining another position, however, working for Dr. Karl Zehnder at a laboratory in Zurich's Canton Hospital.

Meanwhile, the war in Western Europe had turned against the Nazis. By 1944, when Elisabeth went to work at the hospital, German forces were retreating across Europe in the face of a large Allied force, led by American, French, and British troops. The fighting drove many villagers out of their homes, and refugees streamed across the Swiss border seeking safety. Dressed shabbily and suffering from starvation, some of the refugees sought help at Canton Hospital. Somehow, they were directed to Elisabeth's laboratory, and she soon found herself running a refugee program to care for them. The empathy that Elisabeth had demonstrated toward her wounded animals was now applied to the women and children who arrived at her laboratory. She even went around Zurich, gathering up food and clothing from local residents, to bring to the refugees.

While she was tending to the refugees' needs, Elisabeth also carried on her regular duties at the laboratory. One day, as she worked, a piece of laboratory equipment suddenly exploded, seriously burning her face and hands. Although she was treated at the hospital and the skin restored by plastic surgery, the doctors believed that she would never be able to use her hands in medical work. Elisabeth refused to accept what they had said. With the help of a friend and coworker, named Baldwin, she determined to regain the full use of her hands. As her biographer Derek Gill explained, she worked out on "a system of pulleys and weights [designed by Baldwin]. Every evening that followed, and until she fell asleep, Elisabeth worked on stretching the tissue of her hands.... The new skin on the back of her hands began to stretch, the joints to loosen."

Still the doctors were convinced that she would not fully regain the use of her hands. She was invited to a class at the hospital, conducted by the plastic surgeon who had restored her skin. "The wounds, he noted [to the students], had healed well, but, he added, the patient's fingers would be permanently inflexible. Thereupon, in spite of the stab of pain caused by stretching the pearly white and glistening new skin, Elisabeth fully opened and closed her fingers. The professor's jaw sagged. Elisabeth and Baldwin relished their moment of triumph."[8]

Following the end of the war in Europe in May 1945, Elisabeth decided to take a short leave from Canton Hospital during the summer months and work with the International Voluntary Service for Peace (IVSP) in France, rebuilding the country. Her father was strongly opposed to Elisabeth's plan. He feared that she might be killed by land mines placed there by the retreating Germans. Nevertheless, Elisabeth decided to go without his approval. With a group of other volunteers, she went to the village of Ecurcey. There she cooked for the other members of the Voluntary Service and worked alongside them, rebuilding houses in Ecurcey. After the summer was over, Elisabeth returned to Zurich, where she passed the exams to become a laboratory technician.

In 1946, Elisabeth obtained a new job at the University of Zurich, working for Professor Marc Amsler, a well-known opthalmalogist (eye doctor). He had developed techniques to help patients with severe eye problems avoid complete blindness. Elisabeth found herself, as his assistant, counseling patients and helping them deal with the fears they experienced over losing their eyesight. Therefore, she had become more than a laboratory technician; she had also become a valued counselor who empathized with the feelings of her patients.

TRAVELING TO POLAND

Although she found her new work challenging, Elisabeth never forgot her vow to go to Poland. Through the IVSP, she met a young American named David Ritchie. David was planning to go to Poland and promised to help Elisabeth get there once he arrived. In 1947, she finally received a telegram from him: "Come to Poland as soon as possible. Greatly needed. Letter follows."[9] The letter explained that Elisabeth was to take a ship to Gdansk, Poland, then travel to Warsaw by train. There she would meet David Ritchie.

Elisabeth traveled aboard an old steamer across the Baltic Sea, where she met several doctors who were also heading for Poland. After reaching Gdansk, the travelers boarded the train for Warsaw. The passenger cars were so crowded, however, that Elisabeth and the doctors decided to ride part of the way on the roof of one of the cars. It was a harrowing experience. As the train reached a tunnel, Elisabeth had to lie flat on her stomach and hold onto one of the men to avoid being killed. She had "a vivid picture in her mind of five headless people, their arms still intertwined, arriving at Warsaw!"[10] But she survived the trip without injury.

Once in Warsaw, she met David Ritchie, who took her to the town of Lucima. There she worked with two women,

Hanka and Danka, who ran a small health clinic. One night, Elisabeth was awakened by a woman who had brought a sick child to the clinic. The child was suffering from typhoid fever, a serious disease that Elisabeth could not treat at the clinic. The woman insisted that Elisabeth do something. As she told her, this little boy was the last of their 13 children. The others had been killed by the Nazis at a concentration camp.

Elisabeth helped the woman carry the little boy to Lublin, the nearest city, where there was a hospital that could treat him. The doctor at first refused to help, believing that typhoid was fatal and the boy could not be saved. Elisabeth would not take no for an answer. "I will go back to Switzerland," she told him, "and tell everybody the Poles are the most hard-hearted people, that they have no love or compassion, and that a Polish doctor had no empathy for a woman whose child, the last of 13, survived a concentration camp." [11] Finally, the doctor agreed to treat the child. Three weeks later, he had been cured.

While she was working in Poland, Elisabeth decided to visit the former Nazi concentration camp at Maidanek. During World War II, more than 300,000 people—mainly Jews—were killed there by the Nazis. As she walked through the remains of the death camp, Elisabeth entered the barracks, where people lived their final days before going to the gas chambers. Some had left their names carved on the walls. What struck Elisabeth as more unusual, though, were the butterflies that prisoners had drawn on the walls. Later, the butterfly would become the symbol of her work with the dying. Indeed, she wrote that the experience of visiting Maidenek helped persuade her to work in the field of thanatology (the study of death and dying). (For more information on the Maidanek camp, enter "Maidanek concentration camp" into any search engine and browse the sites listed.)

After working in Poland, Elisabeth returned to the eye clinic run by Dr. Amsler. She continued to counsel patients during 1949. Although Elisabeth enjoyed the work, she had never given up her dream of becoming a physician. She began to save her money for medical school and to study for the exams that she had to pass to be accepted into a program. It took her the next two years to prepare herself. In September 1951, Elisabeth finally took the examinations, called the Mature. Near the end of the month, she received a letter: "The examiners are pleased to announce that Elisabeth Kübler has passed the Mature!" Finally, her dream of becoming a doctor was about to be realized.

3 Dr. Kübler-Ross

In 1951, Elisabeth Kübler entered medical school at the University of Zurich. She began a challenging seven and one-half year course of study that was required for anyone who wanted to become a doctor. During the first year, Kübler studied basic subjects, such as chemistry and physics. Over the next two years, she focused on more specialized courses necessary for doctors, such as anatomy and pathology—the causes of death in patients. After passing examinations to demonstrate her knowledge of these subjects, Kübler then spent the last part of her medical studies on more advanced work, including the care of sick patients.

It was an extremely challenging program, and even more so for Kübler, because she received no financial help from her father. He still refused to recognize his daughter's desire to become a doctor and expected her to join him in the office supply business. Fortunately, in Switzerland at that time college tuition expenses were paid by the government, and Kübler was only responsible for paying the cost of books and school supplies. She continued her job at the laboratory with Professor Amsler, working there in the evenings after a long day of classes. Part of what she earned went to pay the cost of an apartment, because Kübler refused to live at home with her parents. She shared the rent with an old friend, Cilly Hofmeyr, a speech therapist in Zurich.

ELISABETH KÜBLER MEETS HER FUTURE HUSBAND
Kübler and Hofmeyr regularly held open house at their apartment for other medical students who were attending the University of Zurich. Many of the students there came from foreign countries, including France, Austria, and the United States. Kübler had learned some English during the time she spent working for the Volunteers. She also spoke French, as well as German. During her anatomy class, she met a tall, friendly medical student from New York named Emanuel Ross. Born in Brooklyn, Manny had lived in a poor Jewish

neighborhood. Both his parents were deaf-mutes. He had enlisted in the Navy in 1946, and after his discharge, the GI Bill (a tuition program for people who had served in the Armed Forces) paid for his college education at New York University. After graduation, Manny decided to attend medical school. Unfortunately, there were no openings in the United States, so he came to Zurich.

With the little time that she had left over after school and her part-time job, Kübler began seeing more and more of Ross. They presented quite a contrast—the tiny Swiss medical student and her big, broad-shouldered American companion. Kübler was an accomplished skier, but Ross had never been on skis in his life. He learned quickly from Seppli Bucher, a skiing champion who had married Kübler's sister, Eva. Ross was welcomed by Kübler's parents, especially her father, who enjoyed talking with him about politics, literature, philosophy, and mountain climbing.

As her medical studies continued, Kübler excelled in many of her courses. Among her favorites was forensic pathology, the branch of medicine concerned with the causes of death among murder victims. She enjoyed examining an organ from the victim's body and then trying to figure out how the murder had been committed. For a while, she even considered entering the field of forensic pathology after graduation, but her interests gradually moved elsewhere.

As part of her medical training, Kübler took over a small practice for another doctor who had been called into the armed forces in 1956. It was a country practice, and the doctor traveled the hilly roads between small villages on a motorcycle to visit his patients. Since Kübler did not even know how to drive a car, the motorcycle became quite a challenge. During her first attempt at driving it, the motorcycle hit a pothole and she flew off the seat onto the side of the road. Fortunately, the incident had been witnessed by several farmers, who picked her up and made sure she wasn't seriously hurt.

A lady doctor was quite unusual in the Swiss countryside, but Kübler soon developed a reputation as a skilled healer. Among her patients was an elderly woman who was dying. Kübler was struck by how calmly she accepted her death as the natural end of a long life. By contrast, she treated a young blacksmith who was dying of lung cancer. The man was angry at being struck down in the prime of life and worried about the wife and children he was soon to leave behind. From these two patients, Kübler increased her understanding of death and dying—a learning process that had begun many years earlier.

BECOMING A DOCTOR

In 1957, Kübler began taking her final examinations to become a doctor. The exams covered the wide range of courses that she had taken during medical school, including surgery, forensic medicine, pediatrics (the study of childhood diseases), and psychiatry. Meanwhile, a tragedy was developing in Kübler's own family. Her sister's husband, Seppli Bucher, had been diagnosed with what the doctors thought was an ulcer. However, they wanted to do exploratory surgery to confirm their diagnosis. Kübler participated in the surgery, which revealed not only an ulcer, but cancer. The disease had progressed so far that the doctors could do nothing to save Bucher, who was only twenty-eight years old. As she helped her sister care for Bucher, Kübler finished her medical exams. Then she waited anxiously for the results. Finally, she received word from the chief medical examiner at the University: "You have passed. You are a physician." [13]

By this time, Ross and Kübler had decided to be married. Ross wanted to return to the United States, but Kübler was not so sure. She had imagined herself practicing among the poor in Africa or India. During the few months before the marriage ceremony, Kübler ran a small medical practice in the countryside outside of Zurich. One day she looked out the window of her office and saw geese flying overhead. In her journal, she wrote: "How do these geese know when to fly to the sun? Who tells them the seasons? How do we, humans, know when it is time to move on? How do we know when to go? As with the migrant birds, so surely with us, there is a voice within, if only we would listen to it, that tells us so certainly when to go forth into the unknown." [14]

LEAVING HOME FOR THE UNITED STATES

Elisabeth Kübler-Ross decided to go to the United States following her wedding, but it was difficult for her to leave behind everyone she knew in Zurich—friends, family, professors, and a way of life that was so familiar to her. New York, she quickly discovered, was entirely different. In Brooklyn, he met Ross's family, and they lived there with his brother and sister-in-law while they looked for their own apartment. Kübler-Ross had to become familiar with English, a language that she did not entirely understand. She and Ross also had to adjust to the grueling schedule of working as interns at Glen Cove Community Hospital, where both of them had obtained appointments. Interns are expected to put in long hours and get little sleep. Every other weekend, Ross and Kübler-Ross were also expected to be available at the hospital around the clock to care for the patients. There was very little time for recreation, although they did occasionally attend cocktail parties among the staff. Kübler-Ross did not enjoy them, partly because she couldn't always understand what people were saying to her. "Last evening," she wrote her sister Erika, "I spent 10 minutes trying to understand what a nurse was talking about when she invited me to attend a baby shower! Why should I want to look at a bathroom constructed for infants? It turns out that a baby shower is a gift party for a pregnant woman." [15]

In 1958, the internships at Glen Cove Hospital were over. The next step in a doctor's training is called a residency. Ross had decided to specialize in the field of pathology and went to work as a resident at Montefiore Hospital in the Bronx.

Kübler-Ross applied for a position in pediatric medicine at Columbia Presbyterian Medical Center in New York City, one of the area's most prestigious hospitals. Because of the long hours expected of residents, Kübler-Ross was told that the hospital could not accept any women who were planning to become pregnant and have children. She agreed to postpone having a family and was given a position at Columbia Presbyterian. Soon afterward, however, she became pregnant and had to turn down the residency. Although the pregnancy eventually ended in a miscarriage, Kübler-Ross did not have time to reapply to Columbia Presbyterian.

Instead, she applied for a position at Manhattan State Hospital, which treated the poor who suffered from mental illness. She began working as a resident there in 1959. What Kübler-Ross found at the State Hospital profoundly disturbed her. Many patients seemed to be treated primarily with strong drugs that were designed to keep them quiet rather than provide them with long-term help. Kübler-Ross began giving patients individual counseling that might help them get better and leave the hospital. She also helped start programs that organized volunteers from the community to come to the hospital and visit patients, giving them more contact with the outside world. As some patients prepared to leave the hospital, Kübler-Ross took them on shopping trips, so they could learn to manage their own money outside the hospital.

While at Manhattan State Hospital, Kübler-Ross took particular interest in a young female patient named Rachel. During her stay at the hospital, Rachel had refused to speak a single word. Kübler-Ross sat with Rachel and tried to encourage her to talk. On her birthday, she made a cake for the celebration. Still Rachel refused to communicate, and Kübler-Ross's boss told her to give up on the young woman. She refused. One day as they were sitting together, Kübler-Ross said to her: "All you have to do is to speak one word, and then we'll travel together until your health is fully restored. If you understand what I'm saying, answer me with one word. Simply say, 'Yes'."[16] After a long hesitation, Rachel spoke that single word. From that time onward, she continued to improve, and she finally left the hospital.

In 1960, while still working at Manhattan State, Kübler-Ross gave birth to a son, whom she and her husband named Kenneth. Soon afterward, they hired an experienced nanny to care for Kenneth, and Kübler-Ross returned to her residency. The following year, she completed her work at Manhattan State and took a position as a resident in psychiatry at Montefiore Hospital, where her husband worked. Unfortunately, Kübler-Ross's work was soon interrupted by a telegram from her mother in Switzerland announcing that Mr. Kübler was dying. Kübler-Ross rushed home and found him in a hospital in Zurich. Mr. Kübler realized that he had very little time to live and asked to be taken home. The doctors refused, because they felt responsible for him and wanted their patient to remain in the hospital. Only when Kübler-Ross agreed to take full responsibility for her father were the doctors willing to release him. She had obtained medical equipment to care for him at home as well as a nurse to assist her. Once he arrived there, Kübler-Ross recalled, he was much happier. "Home at last," he said.[17]

Any conflicts between Kübler-Ross and Mr. Kübler had been forgotten. Instead, they talked about philosophy and religion. He lasted only a few more days, but during that time he was surrounded by his family. From her experience with her father's death, as well as from her work counseling dying patients as a resident at Montefiore, Kübler-Ross had gradually added to her understanding of death and the needs of terminally ill patients.

MOVING TO COLORADO

Her next job gave Kübler-Ross an unusual opportunity to use this knowledge. She and Ross received appointments at the

University of Colorado School of Medicine in Denver in 1962. By this time, Kübler-Ross had become "Americanized," as she called it. "I chewed gum, I ate hamburgers and sugary breakfast cereals...." [18] The only thing, she said, that was difficult for her to understand was the American focus on money. "If people have money, they are considered important and successful. If they don't, they're not." [19] Colorado reminded her far more than New York City of the land she had left behind in Switzerland. With its snowy peaks, rolling hills, and deep valleys, Colorado looked like the mountainsides that Kübler-Ross had hiked with her father when she was a girl.

At the University, Kübler-Ross worked with mentally ill adults and children. She found that counseling children was especially satisfying, and many of her patients showed tremendous improvement. During her work at the University, she was strongly influenced by one of the professors, Dr. Sydney Margolin. "He has the best mind I've ever encountered," she wrote. "This is the man who is going to be my teacher." [20] She was right. One day, Dr. Margolin informed Kübler-Ross that he was supposed to lecture to a group of students but had to leave Denver for another appointment. He asked her to fill in for him.

This assignment was a great compliment to Kübler-Ross, but it was also an enormous challenge for a young doctor. Trying to hold the attention of a group of demanding medical students in a lecture hall was extremely difficult. Kübler-Ross eventually decided that an effective way of doing so would be to speak on an unusual topic—death. Most physicians did not like to focus on the dying, because these were patients that could not be helped. Doctors prided themselves on their ability to help the sick and find cures for them. Kübler-Ross decided that her lecture would consist of a discussion about the role of death and funeral practices in various cultures. Then, she planned to bring in a young dying patient to share with the class her feelings about terminal illness.

The young patient, suffering from leukemia (a type of cancer), was a teenager named Linda. Elisabeth had begun counseling Linda, who was angry about her fate. Linda also felt isolated because no one around her—not family, friends, or physicians—wanted to talk about her impending death. Kübler-Ross proved to be the exception. As a result, Linda agreed to participate in the lecture. At first, the medical students were reluctant to discuss Linda's terminal illness. When Kübler-Ross began asking Linda about her feelings, and the young woman described how she felt about her coming death and the attitudes of the other people around her, however, some of the medical students gradually felt comfortable enough to join in the discussion. This helped them understand the needs of a dying patient as well as their own feelings about death. At the end of the lecture, Kübler-Ross told them, "Maybe now you'll not only know how a dying patient feels, but you'll also be able to treat them with compassion, the same compassion that you'd want for yourself."[21]

Scenes from the Life of Elisabeth Kübler-Ross

Brother Ernst with the Kübler triplets. An old family story has it that even the Küblers found it so difficult to tell Erika and Elisabeth apart that sometimes one of them was bathed twice and the other not at all. When they were older and in school, sometimes one would take a test for the other on a subject the other did not know very well.

Elisabeth, Eva, and Erika Kübler. Mrs. Kübler dressed the triplets in matching outfits and paraded them through the park, where they were always the center of attention. Mr. Kübler, proud of the triplets, allowed the girls to appear on billboards advertising soap and food products.

The Kübler family on a ski trip when the triplets were 8 years old. Mr. Kübler was an avid skier and a member of the prestigious Zurick Ski Club and reveled in these family outings. His favorite pastimes were hiking, mountain climbing, and skiing. Mrs. Kübler was also an advanced skier.

Elisabeth with her friend Cilly Hofmeyr. She and Cilly shared an apartment on Seefeldstrasse while attending medical school. Elisabeth was sorry to have to give up the apartment, to save money, and move back in with her parents. As she told Cilly, leaving their apartment was like "yielding up your own castle and kingdom." It was in that apartment that she achieved total independence.

Professor Marc Amsler's laboratory in the ophthalmology department at the University of Zurich provided Elisabeth with employment shortly after she earned her certificate as a laboratory technician. There, Elisabeth began working in her darkroom lab with patients to discover diseases linked to their eye abnormalities. Amsler appreciated her help so much that he eventually requested her help during surgery.

The young Dr. Elisabeth Kübler. In fall 1956, during her senior year of medical school, Elisabeth did an internship as a country doctor. There, she took over for the attending physician, working 7 days a week. She performed lab tests and on the side learned to ride a vintage motorcycle. Prior to this time she had not even obtained a driver's license! Though she looked little older than a teenager, the villagers gave her a warm reception and encouragement.

Manny Ross, an American, as a medical student in Zurich. Elisabeth and Manny met at the university, where she found herself serving as translator for several of the American students there. She invited Manny and two of his friends to have dinner at her home over a Christmas holiday and thereafter, Manny became a regular visitor.

Elisabeth and Manny were married in a civil ceremony on February 7, 1958. Her mother insisted on having a wedding banquet after the ceremony and a downpour of rain doused the wedding party and their guests while they ran from their cars to the restaurant.

Manny and Elisabeth with their son Kenneth, just a few days old, in their Bronx apartment in July, 1960. After several miscarriages, Elisabeth successfully delivered Kenneth when he was almost a month overdue. Her mother stayed to help with the baby for 2 weeks and was replaced by a Swiss nursemaid who allowed Elisabeth to continue with her medical residency.

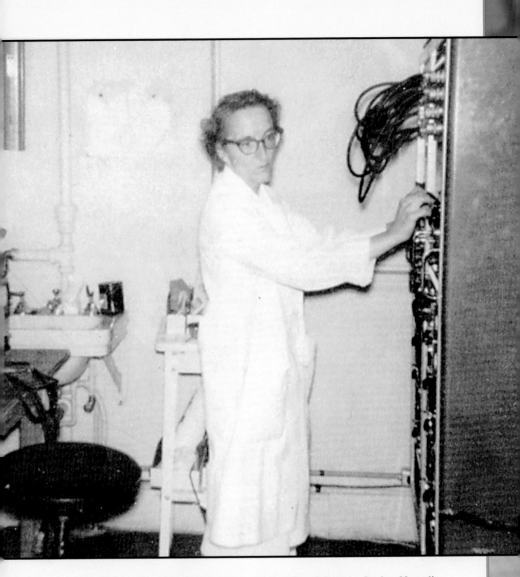

Elisabeth in Dr. Margolin's lab at the University of Denver. Seeing Margolin
lecture for the first time, Elisabeth said, "He has the best mind I have ever
encountered ... This is the man who is going to be my teacher. Dr. Margolin
is surely the reason I'm in Denver!" She lost no time in securing a position
as an assistant in his lab, where she began working in July 1963.

Elisabeth's children, Barbara and Kenneth, at the Chicago train station where they waited for their mother to come home from work. Elisabeth gave birth to Barbara in a difficult delivery and after suffering several miscarriages. She took the three-pound baby home to nurse her around the clock.

Elisabeth in May 1975 after publishing several books on treating dying patients. The books were an offshoot of lectures she gave on the subject and interviews that she had with dying patients. Her lectures compelled nurses, doctors, students, and chaplains to examine their own feelings on death and dying and her work there was not well-received by all of the Billings Hospital staff.

Elisabeth talks with a young leukemia patient, Eva, behind a one-way window. She noted in her journal that every patient she spoke with taught her something new. The patients responded with appreciation and a sense of relief at being allowed to express their feelings.

Elisabeth Kübler-Ross in 2001. Retired and confined to a wheelchair after a series of strokes, she now says, "I am like a plane that has left the gate and not taken off. I would rather go back to the gate or fly away." She lives in Arizona enjoying the daily company of birds and coyotes. She still receives mail from all over the world from those familiar with her work.

4

On Death
and Dying

The seed that Elisabeth Kübler-Ross planted in Denver began to grow in Chicago, as well. In 1965, Kübler-Ross and her husband took up new positions at the city's leading hospitals; she became assistant professor of psychiatry at the University of Chicago Medical School, where she lectured students. She also counseled patients with psychological problems at Billings Hospital, which was part of the university. One day she received a visit from several students who were attending nearby Chicago Theological Seminary. The students explained that they had read about the seminar on death and dying that Kübler-Ross had conducted in Denver. One of the students added that although they were learning all the religious doctrine necessary to become ministers, no one was teaching them how to counsel the dying.

As a result of this meeting, Kübler-Ross decided to organize a seminar on death and dying for these students at Billings Hospital. To make the seminar effective, however, she needed to find a patient who would talk about his feelings as he neared death. When Kübler-Ross asked some of her colleagues to recommend a patient who might be willing to participate in the seminar, they were appalled. Some of them felt that she would be taking advantage of a terminally ill patient during his or her last weeks of life. Others were clearly uncomfortable even discussing the issue of death.

During the 1960s, some doctors preferred not to tell terminally ill patients that they were, in fact, dying. They believed that the patients were not capable of handling the truth. As Kübler-Ross had discovered in her work with the terminally ill in Colorado, however, most of them knew they were dying, although the doctors had refused to share that information with them. These patients wanted to talk about their feelings with someone who would listen. Instead, the hospital staff seemed reluctant to deal with death. Doctors and nurses were far too busy administering medications, giving the patients transfusions of blood to keep them alive, or providing them with life support on high-tech medical machines. Their job was to use all the modern technology available to them to cure patients or, if that was not possible, to at least keep them alive as long as they could. Medical staffs were uncomfortable confronting death.

Eventually, with the help of a sympathetic colleague, Kübler-Ross found an elderly man who was willing to participate in the seminar. During her first visit with the patient, however, Kübler-Ross made a serious mistake. The patient simply wanted to talk to an understanding doctor, one to one. Instead of doing this, Kübler-Ross was so excited about finding someone for her seminar that she did not listen to him. She told the man that they could talk during the seminar program itself. The following day when she returned, the man had grown so weak that he could no longer participate in the program. As Kübler-Ross approached his bed, he said, "Thank you for trying."[22] These were among his last words before dying. Kübler-Ross realized that in her enthusiasm to put on the seminar, she had failed to help a dying patient.

Shortly afterward, she found another elderly man who agreed to be interviewed in the program. Kübler-Ross elicited his feelings about the experience of dying and, after the seminar had ended and the patient had returned to his room, her students discussed what they had learned.

SEMINARS GROW TO BECOME A PROGRAM

From this initial seminar, the program on death and dying began to grow. It was attended by theological students, social workers, and nurses from Billings Hospital. In each seminar, Kübler-Ross interviewed the dying patient in a screening room. Outside the room, behind a two-way mirror, the students watched, without being seen by the patient.

The students who attended the seminars recognized the importance of helping the terminally ill deal with their feelings as they approached death. They also realized that nothing in their education or training had prepared them to provide this kind of help. As Kübler-Ross said to one of the patients who participated in the program and shared her feelings, you have been "such a very good teacher."[23] The dying patients, themselves, were teaching the students how to assist others who were facing a terminal illness.

American society, Kübler-Ross realized, did not feel comfortable dealing with death. The dying were usually placed in hospitals, away from their families, where they were expected to spend their final days among strangers. She recalled her own experience when, as a child and suffering from pneumonia—a life-threatening childhood illness—she was taken to the hospital by her parents. It was a cold, impersonal environment. The terminally ill felt isolated in a hospital, unable to express their feelings even to doctors and nurses, who tried to avoid the issue of death. Often the patients could not even discuss death with their families. Some family members were far too sad to talk to the patient. Others were afraid of bringing up the topic and upsetting the patient. As a result, the dying felt completely alone.

Kübler-Ross also discovered that many of her students were also uncomfortable discussing the fact of their own death. The seminar helped them to open up and discuss feelings that they had never shared with anyone else. This experience helped them to feel more comfortable with their patients. As Kübler-Ross put it: "If we cannot face death with equanimity, how can we be of assistance to our patients? We, then, hope that our patients will not ask us this horrible question. We make rounds and talk about trivialities or the wonderful weather outside and the sensitive patient will play the game and talk about next spring, even if he is quite aware that there will be no next spring for him."[24]

Kübler-Ross believed strongly that doctors should tell their patients when they are terminally ill. There should be no question of whether or not to say anything. How the information was delivered, however, was most important. As she told the participants in her seminars, "What all our patients stressed was the sense of empathy, which counted more than the immediate tragedy of the news. It was the reassurance that everything possible will be done, that they will not be 'dropped' [forgotten], that there were treatments available, that there was a glimpse of hope—even in the most advanced

The Cleaning Woman

While at Billings Hospital in Chicago, Kübler-Ross recalled that her "greatest teacher" was an African American cleaning woman who worked in the hospital.* Kübler-Ross noticed that the woman would stop in and visit with dying patients and, after she left, the terminally ill seemed to feel much better. Kübler-Ross wanted to know what the woman was saying to help the patients. Eventually, they had a lengthy discussion, and the woman revealed that she had lost a three-year-old son many years earlier. He had developed pneumonia, the woman explained, and she had taken him to a nearby hospital. Many poor people were there, waiting to be treated, and the hospital staff could not treat her son immediately. He died in her arms. "You see, death is not a stranger to me," she told Kübler-Ross. "He is an old, old acquaintance. I'm not afraid of him anymore. Sometimes I walk into the rooms of these patients, and they are simply petrified and have no one to talk to. So I go near them. Sometimes I even touch their hands and tell them not to worry, that it's not so terrible."** Shortly afterward, Kübler-Ross took this woman out of her job cleaning hospital floors and made her a counselor to the dying.

* Elisabeth Kübler-Ross, *The Wheel of Life: A Memoir of Living and Dying*, New York: Scribner, 1997, p. 143.

** Ibid., p. 144.

cases."[25] Unfortunately, none of the doctors at Billings Hospital heard this message. They refused to attend the seminars that Kübler-Ross was conducting. Nevertheless, she continued to expand the seminar program while counseling dying patients at Billings Hospital.

One person, Dr. Renford Gaines, a chaplain at Billings Hospital, agreed to work with Kübler-Ross. During her rounds, some patients expressed spiritual and religious concerns, which she felt unqualified to handle. Gaines was far more experienced in these areas. He not only helped in counseling the terminally ill but also in running the death and dying seminars.

While handling a heavy workload, Kübler-Ross was suddenly struck by another tragedy in her own family. In 1967, her mother suffered a serious stroke in Switzerland. Kübler-Ross rushed to her bedside and found that Mrs. Kübler could only communicate by blinking her eyes. Nevertheless, she told Elisabeth and her sisters that she did not want to stay in the hospital—it was far too impersonal. Instead, they moved her to a small home for the aged, where she had a sunny room with a garden outside of it. Mrs. Kübler remained there for the next four years, until her death.

After returning to Chicago, Kübler-Ross expanded her work. She was asked by the Lutheran Theological Seminary to teach courses to the divinity students. She also worked at a program for the blind, called Lighthouse. She counseled young patients that blindness need not prevent them from holding jobs, having families, and enjoying fulfilling lives. (For more information on Chicago's Lighthouse, enter this name into any search engine and browse the sites listed.)

THE SUCCESS OF *ON DEATH AND DYING*

In 1969, the Chicago Theological Seminary published an article, written by Kübler-Ross, describing her seminars on death and dying. Somehow the article was seen by an editor at a major New York City publishing company. The publisher asked Kübler-Ross to write a short book on death and dying, for which she received a fee of $7,000. Published later that year, *On Death and Dying* became an international best seller. Based on interviews with several hundred patients, it was the first book to talk about the experience of dying among the terminally ill and to explain how caregivers and families patients could deal with death most effectively.

In her book, Kübler-Ross talked about five stages that the dying go through as they approach death. These stages do not always occur progressively, that is, one after the other. A patient may move back and forth between one stage and another as the illness progresses. As the patient goes through these stages, his or her family members may also be passing through them.

The first stage is what Kübler-Ross calls the "No, not me, it cannot be true," phase.[26] A patient who is told that she has terminal lung cancer may first deny that it could be possible. It seems far too incredible that she could be stricken with a fatal illness. The patient's immediate reaction may be that the doctor has made a mistake, that the x-rays taken of her lungs are wrong, or that her blood tests have been mixed up with some other patient's.

As a psychiatrist, Kübler-Ross knew that denial is a natural defense used by people throughout their lives. When tragedy strikes, at first it seems impossible to believe it. For example, if someone is suddenly killed in a freak accident, the first response of family members is disbelief. Kübler-Ross recognized that denial is the way that human beings give themselves a little time to get used to the tragedy. This is also true when a dying patient is told of his or her terminal illness. "Denial functions as a buffer," she wrote, "after unexpected shocking news, allows the patient to collect himself, and with time, mobilize other...defenses. This does not mean, however, that later on the same patient will not be willing or even happy and relieved if he can sit and talk with someone about his impending death. Such a dialogue will and must take place at the convenience of the patient, when he (not the listener!) is ready to face it." [27]

Families and friends of the patient may also experience denial as the first stage of dealing with a terminal illness. They don't want to face reality, especially when the terminally ill patient is a young person or a child. Sometimes denial by family members can prevent the patient from engaging in a meaningful conversation about death that can make it easier to face.

According to Kübler-Ross, a few patients remain locked in the denial stage for the duration of their illness. Most others, however, pass into another phase, when they ask: "Why me?" [28] In this second stage, patients feel angry that they are the ones with a terminal illness. They may even selfishly wish that the illness had struck someone else. Patients frequently take their anger out on the people around them. They may find fault with the hospital staff, yell at family and friends, and even curse God for their illness. Kübler-Ross explained in her book that this is the natural reaction of anyone who is facing death. Many patients feel angry because they seem to be losing control of their lives. Women who fill responsible positions at work suddenly find themselves too weak to go to their offices. Responsible fathers who enjoyed playing with their children lack the strength to participate in these activities any longer. "What is happening to me?" the patients ask themselves.

Caregivers must wait and patiently listen to what the sick person is saying, Kübler-Ross wrote in *On Death and Dying* that frequently this willingness to listen and understand will help terminally ill patients cope with their anger, "A patient who is respected and understood, who is given attention and a little time, will soon lower his voice and reduce his angry demands. He will know that he is a valuable human being, cared for, allowed to function at the highest possible level as long as he can. He will be listened to without the need for a temper tantrum; he will be visited without ringing the bell every so often because dropping in on him is not a necessary duty but a pleasure."[29]

Anger may not entirely disappear. One day a patient may accept his or her inevitable death, whereas at another time, he or she may feel angry that life will soon be ending. In order to prevent the end from coming too soon, patients may enter a third stage of illness. Kübler-Ross calls this the bargaining phase. A patient may try to bargain with God. If God will cure him, then he will promise to be a good person in the future. Even if God will give him a few more years, the patient will agree to dedicate himself to helping other people. Sometimes this bargaining phase can help a patient feel more at peace and even hope for a remarkable recovery, at least for a short time.

Most patients, however, enter another phase, which Kübler-Ross calls depression. During this stage, patients experience an overpowering sense of loss. Some patients feel regret at all the things that they either never accomplished or had left undone in their lives. They look back on lost opportunities in their careers and unpleasant relationships with family members that were never healed. Terminally ill parents with young children must face the fact that they are leaving their families behind them. According to Kübler-Ross, caregivers can help terminally ill patients deal with some of these issues in the time remaining. For example, a husband and his terminally ill wife can discuss the most effective methods of providing for their children after her death. By taking concrete steps to deal with these problems, many patients feel far less anxious about how their families will cope without them.

It is far more difficult for most patients, though, to look forward to the complete loss of self that occurs with death. As

Kübler-Ross wrote, it is natural to feel sad and depressed as such an event approaches:

> The patient should not be encouraged to look at the sunny side of things, as this would mean he should not contemplate his impending death. It would be [incorrect] to tell him not to be sad, since all of us are tremendously sad when we lose one beloved person. The patient is in the process of losing everything and everybody he loves. If he is allowed to express his sorrow, he will find a final acceptance much easier, and he will be grateful to those who can sit with him during this stage of depression without constantly telling him not to be sad.[30]

According to Kübler-Ross, the final stage of terminal illness, at least for some patients, is acceptance. The anger, depression, and sadness slip away, and the patient prepares for death. Kübler-Ross cautions that the patient may not be happy but will probably have few, if any, feelings. Patients may wish to spend most of their time alone. This may be difficult for their families, who may want to be with them and to talk with them as much as possible before they die. "Our communications then become more nonverbal than verbal," Kübler-Ross wrote. "The patient may just make a gesture of the hand to invite us to sit down for a while. He may just hold our hand and ask us to sit in silence....Our presence may just confirm that we are going to be around until the end."[31]

Although patients may accept death, Kübler-Ross points out that they may still possess a lingering hope that a cure is still possible. A new experimental medicine may be discovered that holds out the chance of a miracle. Kübler-Ross emphasizes that physicians should also encourage hope among their patients. "This does not mean that doctors have to tell them a lie," she wrote. "It merely means that we share with them the hope that something unforeseen may happen, that they ... will live longer than is expected."[32] Once patients give up hope, then their death usually occurs within a day.

Shortly after Kübler-Ross's book was published, she was contacted by the editors of *Life* magazine, which was read by millions of people. They wanted to publish an article about her work, with pictures of her counseling a dying patient. Kübler-Ross chose a patient named Eva, a beautiful young woman suffering from leukemia, a type of cancer. Eva talked openly about her anger and her fears. On November 21, 1969, Kübler-Ross and Eva appeared in *Life* and became known to readers throughout the world. Suddenly, Elisabeth Kübler-Ross had become internationally famous.

Children and Death 5

Although Kübler-Ross's book brought her fame, it did not bring her the respect of her colleagues at the University of Chicago. As one of the doctors at the hospital put it, "We have tried for years to make this hospital famous for our excellent cancer care. Now this woman comes along and makes us famous for our dying patients!"[33] The hospital staff then prevented Elisabeth from interviewing any other terminally ill patients at her seminars. Meanwhile, participants in the program stayed away. They were afraid to offend the physicians at the hospital. By the end of 1969, Kübler-Ross decided to leave the University of Chicago, realizing that it was not an environment where her work could be appreciated. That same year, she went to work at La Rabida Children's Hospital in Chicago.

The response to her book, however, had been overwhelming. Thousands of letters poured into her office from caregivers and terminally ill patients who wanted to discuss the issues surrounding death. As a result, Kübler-Ross began holding seminars across the United States to talk about the ideas that she had raised in *On Death and Dying*. Psychologists and members of the clergy who worked with the dying attended these seminars, as did terminally ill patients themselves. Kübler-Ross used her gifts as a psychiatrist and a good listener, letting participants talk. Dying patients expressed their anger at being told they were terminally ill. Some participants discussed experiences with death in their own families, and others talked openly about their own fear of death. As a result of the seminars, participants felt comfortable sharing their feelings with each other and came to a more profound awareness of death and dying.

Meanwhile, Kübler-Ross experienced her own close brush with death. In 1970, her husband, Manny, suffered a heart attack. Although, it was only a mild attack, the experience made a strong impact on the couple. Manny's illness also affected the couple's two small children—Kenneth and Barbara. Although Kübler-Ross wanted to take them into the coronary care unit to visit their father, hospital rules did not permit it.

Kübler-Ross believed strongly that children should be aware of a parent's illness and should also learn how to deal with the issues surrounding death. A child may be forced to deal with the death of a parent, an elderly grandparent, or even a brother or sister. According to Kübler-Ross, very young children generally see death as temporary. That is, they think that the person who died will come back to life. In one of her books, Kübler-Ross recalled what happened when her daughter, aged only four years, buried a pet dog. "She suddenly looked at me and said, 'This is really not so sad. Next spring when your tulips come up, he'll come up again and play with me.'"[34] According to Kübler-Ross, this reassuring belief may help small children cope with death until they are finally old enough to realize that it is final.

Some children also experience guilt feelings about the death of a family member. They may recall getting angry at their mother or sister and wishing she were dead. Then, as if by magic, the person dies. These children need to talk about their sense of guilt and recognize that they had nothing to do with the family member's death. They may also need to share their angry feelings over the death of a parent or other family member. Kübler-Ross recalled one little boy whose father had died at the University of Chicago Hospital. She watched him riding the elevator from one floor to another and writing on pieces of paper, which he dropped to the floor. "When he was gone, I gathered up those scraps, pieced them together, and saw he had written, 'Thanks for killing my dad.'"[35] No one had bothered to talk to him about his father's terminal illness, so he was unprepared when his dad died. The little boy couldn't understand what had happened or how to cope with his overwhelming loss.

THE DEATH OF A CHILD

Children themselves do not escape the terminal illnesses that strike adults. Although Kübler-Ross recognized this fact, she had always found working with terminally ill children extremely difficult. As she said, it reminded her that the same kind of illness might strike one of her own children. In 1969, however, she took a new job with La Rabida Children's Hospital, working with dying children. In this position, she emphasized the importance of listening to the children and letting them participate in the experience of their terminal illness.

Elisabeth Kübler-Ross believed that dying children knew in their hearts about the seriousness of their illness. Therefore, it was important for them to be told by their parents and their physicians. As one woman wrote to Kübler-Ross: "I have watched with sadness parents who could or would not be honest with their children about their cancer. They have missed so much. My son and I talked openly about his death. He was able to tell me, 'I am scared.' I was able to say, 'I know, son, but you won't be.' My son taped messages to those he loved, family and friends. He helped plan his funeral. He gave a few things away to friends before he died. We were left with a great legacy—we are lucky. I hope to be able to help other parents to look at their children, to listen to them, and to learn from them."[36]

For parents and other family members, a child's terminal illness creates an overwhelming sorrow. Kübler-Ross recommended that parents not hold their feelings inside. Instead, she always advised families to share their feelings with the dying child. "Tell them you are sad and sometimes feel so useless that you cannot help more," Kübler-Ross wrote in her book *On Children and Death*. "They will hold you in their little arms and feel good that they can help you by sharing comfort. Shared sorrow is much easier to bear than leaving them with feelings of guilt and fear that they are the cause of all your anxiety."[37] Siblings should also be involved in caring for a terminally ill child, according to Kübler-Ross. But she also warned that they should not be forced to give up enjoyment of their own lives.

She emphasized that a home should be a place of joy and laughter, even when a terminally ill child is living there. It cheers up the patient.

During her seminars, Kübler-Ross often talked with the families of terminally ill children. Siblings sometimes felt jealous because the dying child was receiving so much attention. They also experienced guilt for wishing that the ordeal would end so the rest of the family could resume its normal life. These natural feelings were discussed by Kübler-Ross during the seminars so the siblings of a dying child could understand that these feelings were natural and could feel better about them.

The parents of a terminally ill child experienced a wide range of emotions during the course of the illness and after the child's death. Indeed, parents often passed through the same stages that Kübler-Ross described in her book *On Death and Dying*. At first, parents may try to deny that the child has a terminal illness. Then they might wonder why their child had been singled out for such a terrible fate. As one mother recalled: "When the doctors discussed my eleven-year-old daughter's diagnosis with me almost a year ago, my whole world shattered as I tried to figure out why cancer had struck. I knew that I had to try to alter the original prognosis of six months."[38] Hoping for a better diagnosis, this mother took her child to New York. There the doctors prescribed extensive chemotherapy—drugs designed to kill the cancer. This treatment usually makes patients very sick, and this child was no exception. Many patients also lose their hair during chemotherapy treatments. As they grow weaker, they are also unable to do the things that most children enjoy. Terminally ill patients can no longer play sports, they may be unable to do any schoolwork, and eventually they are too weak to leave their beds.

Kübler-Ross recommended that parents deal with these small losses as they occur. "When all these losses can be mourned as they occur," she wrote, "the final grief work will be minimal."[39] She also urged parents to listen closely to the needs of their dying children as they go through treatment and let them participate in their own care.

LOSING A CHILD: THE STAGES OF GRIEF

In her seminars on death and dying, Kübler-Ross helped many parents work through the stages of grief that accompany the

Jeffy

One of Elisabeth Kübler-Ross's patients was a nine-year-old boy named Jeffy. His doctors had given him extensive chemotherapy, which caused him to grow very weak. His illness had not been stopped, however. When the hospital recommended additional chemotherapy, Kübler-Ross convinced Jeffy's parents to let her ask him whether he wanted to continue with the treatment. Jeffy said no. What he really wanted to do was to go home before he died. His parents listened and took him home. There, Jeffy insisted on riding the bicycle that his father had bought him. His parents were fearful that Jeffy was too weak, that he might injure himself by falling off the bicycle. With Kübler-Ross's help, however, his parents decided to let Jeffy try. He mounted the bicycle and rode off, returning later, proud of the fact that he had been able to ride that bicycle. Jeffy then went up to his bedroom to recover from the ride. A short time later, he asked to see his brother Dougy after he came home from school. As his mother explained: "In his bedroom, Jeffy ... told his brother that he wanted the pleasure of personally giving him his most beloved bicycle. But he could not wait another two weeks until Dougy's birthday because by then he would be dead. Therefore he wanted to give it to him now."* Jeffy died soon afterward.

* Elisabeth Kübler-Ross, *The Wheel of Life: A Memoir of Living and Dying,* New York: Scribner, 1997, p. 185.

loss of a child. These are similar to the phases that a dying patient experiences. At first, some parents go through denial. They wish that the child could somehow reappear, that they could hear his voice, see his smile, cheer at his soccer game, and help him with his homework. Parents may feel angry that their child has been taken from them, and blame themselves, believing that somehow they should have been able to do more. One grandparent, who was angry at the loss of his grandson, went into his workshop to deal with his feelings. He vigorously sawed pieces of wood and hammered them together with nails to build a little casket for his grandson's body.

Grieving also involves feelings of depression at the tragic sense of loss when a child dies. According to Kübler-Ross, part of the grieving process is the need to reach out to that dead child, even though he is gone. Some parents dream about their children in the weeks following their death. This helps them deal with the profound sorrow they feel at the loss of a child. Parents also need to talk about their loss with each other, as well as with relatives and friends. There is no prescribed length to the grieving process. Final acceptance of a child's death may take a few months or much longer.

During the early 1970s, Kübler-Ross participated in 700 programs around the issues of death and dying. As a result of these experiences, in 1974 she published *Questions and Answers on Death and Dying*. In this book, she emphasized that doctors should tell their patients as soon as possible when they have been diagnosed with a serious illness. However, she also cautioned that they should be told that the illness is terminal only when they are ready to discuss their own death. Generally, this is the responsibility of the physician. Nevertheless, Kübler-Ross recognized that some doctors were unable to tell their patients that they were dying.

In such a case, another caregiver, such as a social worker or member of the clergy, should ask the doctor's permission to talk to the patient about death. This discussion may be even more difficult if a child or teenager is terminally ill. In fact, the child's parents may not want to raise the subject with their dying daughter or son. Then, Kübler-Ross recommended that a caregiver say: "'Wouldn't it help if you expressed some of your concerns and feelings with your son?' If they are unable to do so, don't push, but at least share with them some of your ... experiences. When this has been done, this may encourage them to open up."[40]

Kübler-Ross emphasized that family and caregivers can help patients through the various stages of dying—from denial to acceptance. Some patients remain in the denial stage longer than others. Caregivers must listen to a patient who may be dying and still believes firmly that a miracle is about to occur and she will be cured. Let the patient tell you his feelings, Kübler-Ross wrote, and don't push him out of the denial stage until he is ready to stop denying reality. When a patient expresses anger—"Why Me?"—caregivers can only sit and let the patient express her anger. Then the patient can also be told that every effort will be made to find some way to stop the illness and save his life. Kübler-Ross recognized that patients should not give up hope, because this only increases the fear and pain. Some patients also live in several stages— anger, bargaining, depression—simultaneously, moving back and forth from one to another before accepting the reality of their illness. Kübler-Ross wrote,

> I think most of our patients would reach the stage of acceptance if it were not for the members of the helping professions, especially the physicians, who cannot accept the death of a patient. If we as physicians have the need to prolong life unnecessarily and to postpone death, the patient often regresses into the state of depression and anger again and is unable to die in peace and acceptance. The second and ... more frequent problem is the immediate family, which 'hangs on' and cannot 'let go.'[41]

In some cases, death occurs suddenly. For example, a child may drown in an accident at a swimming pool or be fatally injured while driving a car. Parents, siblings, and friends may have no time to adjust to a terminal illness, which may make acceptance even more difficult. "If it is a sudden death, and the child's family has had no preparation, this family sometimes needs years of working through the grief," Kübler-Ross wrote.[42] At first, parents and family members need time to deal with the intense shock at realizing the child is dead and the desire to deny that it could possibly happen. Gradually, over the days and weeks ahead, the family members should be encouraged to discuss their feelings, accept them, and begin to adjust to the tragedy of death.

In a letter to parents who have experienced the loss of a child, Kübler-Ross wrote,

> The first few days after the death and the funeral will be busy ones. There are so many things to think of, so many relatives to [deal with] ... so much mail to be answered. ... It is after the ... friends and relatives have gone that the loneliness and real grief begin. At this time, be good to yourself. Don't expect your grief to last forever or to be done in a certain time. In fact, don't think at all. Go through your days as best you can. Cry when you need to cry, beat the pillow if you need to express your anger.... You are entitled to grieve.[43]

In her book *Questions and Answers on Death and Dying,* Kübler-Ross also discussed the most comfortable place for patients to die. She believed that most patients wanted to die at home where, they were surrounded by family members, a spouse, and children, instead of in a hospital, where a patient can only be visited at certain hours of the day. She also emphasized that "children should share these last few weeks or days" with a dying parent.[44]

In her book *Death, The Final Stage of Growth,* published in 1975, Kübler-Ross recalled an experience that occurred when she was a child. A farmer who lived nearby had fallen out of a tree and suffered an injury that was so severe that his life could not be saved. In the little time left to him, he asked to be put in his bed at home. From there he talked with his children, as well as close friends and neighbors, such as Elisabeth Kübler and her sisters. Meanwhile, in his last hours, he could look out of the bedroom window and enjoy the beautiful countryside that was part of his farm. This experience helped him to accept his death. It also helped his children accept the death of their father.

Life After Death 6

As Elisabeth Kübler-Ross continued her work in death and dying, she gradually developed a strong belief in everlasting life. As Kübler-Ross herself admitted, she was not a religious person and did not have a faith in God or in life after death. However, interviews with hundreds and hundreds of patients changed her mind. One patient had been brought into a hospital from a terrible car accident and pronounced dead on arrival. Much to the surprise of her doctors, she came back to life. The patient reported that while she was "dead" she had met her husband, who had been killed in another car crash, miles away. A short time later, his death was confirmed. How could this woman have known about her husband's death, Kübler-Ross asked herself, unless she had seen him in another world?

A similar incident involved a Native American woman who had been the victim of a fatal hit-and-run accident, 700 miles from her home. Before she died, the woman told a truck driver who stopped to help her that she had already seen her father. After her death, the truck driver found out from her mother that the woman's father had indeed died from a massive heart attack, an hour before the hit-and-run accident. How could the woman have been aware of her father's death hundreds of miles away, Kübler-Ross wondered, unless she had really seen him in the next life?

Kübler-Ross also talked to young children in hospitals who had been brought into emergency rooms after their entire families had been involved in tragic fires or automobile accidents. "I would always sit with the youngest child. When they were nearing death, they would always say something like, 'Mommy and Peter are waiting for me.' The children were never wrong. They never said that a person who survived the accident or the fire was there. It was always, always, always the people who had died."[45] Once incident recalled by Kübler-Ross involved a child who neared death and claimed to see his brother waiting for him. The brother, a victim of the same accident and expected by the medical professionals to live, died, too, only a short time later. When she was told of the brother's death, Kübler-Ross replied, "'Yes, I know,' and they looked at me like I was kookie."[46]

THE PHASES OF DEATH

Her interviews with people who had "died" but then come back to life led Kübler-Ross to propose that death was not the end of everything. Instead, there were various phases of death, different stages that people experienced as they entered the afterlife. In the first phase, according to Kübler-Ross, people hovered above their bodies. They could even hear what others were saying about them after they had "died." In the second phase, Kübler-Ross wrote that patients said they had been transformed into spirits that knew no earthly restrictions. The spirit could move with the speed of light to be with family and friends who were mourning them.

In phase three, patients reported going through a tunnel toward an overpowering light. This was the light of love, which many thought was radiated by God. This love gave them a feeling of great comfort that they had experienced nowhere on earth. Finally, in phase four, they came into the presence of God or what some called the Highest Source. "They experienced a oneness, a completeness of existence," Kübler-Ross wrote. "In this state, people went through a life review, a process in which they confronted the totality of their lives. They went over every action, word, and thought of their lives. They were made to understand the reasons for every decision, thought, and action they had in life. They saw how their actions affected other people, including strangers. They saw what their lives could have been like, the potential they had. They were shown that everybody's life is intertwined, that every thought and action has a kind of ripple effect on every other living thing on the planet."[47]

LIFE AFTER DEATH

Kübler-Ross's ideas on life after death were strongly doubted by many other scientists. As she herself admitted, they probably thought she had "seen too many dying patients. She's slipped." Nevertheless, at one of her workshops in 1975, she told participants, "I know for a fact that there is life after death." Meanwhile, Kübler-Ross had also begun to believe in "channeling." In this process a "channeler" puts himself into a trance in front of a group of people and summons up a dead spirit from the past, who speaks through the "channeler." Indeed, it was a "channeler" in Santa Barbara, California, who, according to Kübler-Ross, urged her to begin lecturing on life after death.

In her autobiography, *The Wheel of Life* (1999), Kübler-Ross described other spirits whom she had seen during channeling.

The Butterfly

Elisabeth Kübler-Ross adopted the butterfly as the symbol of the transition from death to life after death. Like the butterfly, humans spend much of their lives in a cocoon—the human body. At death, they shed the human body, the cocoon, and are transformed into a beautiful butterfly. The butterfly flies off, leaving the cocoon behind, much as the human being leaves the body, and the spirit flies off to life after death. Kübler-Ross used the image of the butterfly in her workshops and in her counseling with individuals who were dying. Many patients seemed to take heart as they listened to her talk about life after death. Children could visualize themselves being transformed into butterflies who left the cocoon of their earthly bodies and entered into a spiritual world after they died. The experience of the butterfly also helped parents of dying children to accept their loss and continue with their lives.

One of them was a tall Native American, named Salem. He appeared in a magnificent robe, and wore a turban on his head. He addressed Kübler-Ross as a woman named Isabel. Salem explained that she had been a teacher, Isabel, 2,000 years earlier, when Jesus Christ was alive. Salem also knew that Kübler-Ross's favorite song was "Always," which was something that she had told no one except her husband.

Kübler-Ross's husband, however, was extremely skeptical of channeling and believed that people who claimed to summon up spirits were fakes. He also did not share his wife's beliefs in an afterlife. This conflict between Kübler-Ross and her husband arose at a time when their marriage had already become very stressful. In part, the strain was caused by her demanding travel schedule. She was appearing regularly around the world, running workshops on death and dying. As a result, she was away from home much of the time, leaving her two children in the care of her husband.

In 1976, Manny Ross finally announced that he no longer wanted to be married and asked for a divorce. Their son and daughter remained with him, and Kübler-Ross left Chicago to live in San Diego. It was an extremely difficult decision. She was ending a marriage that had lasted for 20 years and leaving two young people, whom she dearly loved, behind her. For a time, Elisabeth Kübler-Ross was so upset that she could no longer work.

KÜBLER-ROSS OPENS *SHANTI NILAYA*

Soon after reaching San Diego, however, Kübler-Ross began to develop an idea that would take her life in a new direction. She decided to establish her own healing center, where she could run workshops. With financial help from her former husband, as part of their divorce settlement, Kübler-Ross purchased a piece of property in southern California. "It was a plateau of 42 acres," she wrote, "on top of a mountain, surrounded by a circle of boulder-covered mountains. We saw a beautiful blue sky above, orange trees, an occasional avocado tree, wild lilac bushes...."[48]

In 1977, Kübler-Ross opened her healing center, which she called *Shanti Nilaya,* a Sanscrit word which means "the final home of peace." A large crowd gathered for the celebration, which occurred as the sun rose over southern California on Thanksgiving Day, November 27, 1977. Two participants with trumpets played a song called "The Impossible Dream," because the idea of a healing center had looked impossible only a year earlier. Others sang and played their own songs, while Kübler-Ross auctioned off pillows she had knitted as well as candles she had made to help pay for the celebration.

At Shanti Nilaya, Kübler-Ross and her staff conducted week-long programs, which she called Life, Death, and Transition workshops. Groups of approximately 20 people came to Shanti Nilaya to live and participate in these retreats. Many of the participants were touched by issues of death and dying. Some were terminally ill patients, trying to come to terms with their illness. Others were caring for a dying child or had recently lost a son or daughter. There were also professional caregivers—doctors, nurses, social workers, and members of the clergy.

In addition, some of the participants were trying to deal with what Kübler-Ross called the unfinished business of life. They were experiencing sadness over the way they had been treated as children, over their treatment by a spouse, or over a recent divorce. As Kübler-Ross wrote, "if we have the strength and the courage to confront our own emotions and to accept every one of them as a part of us, we cannot only finish our 'unfinished business,' but ... add months and even years to our lives."[49]

The workshops encouraged people who might never have been allowed to express anger as children to finally come to terms with the natural angry feelings they might have experienced toward family members and friends. Indeed, much of the work of the terminally ill was coming to terms with the anger they felt about dying. Grief is another emotion that all human beings share. In her workshops, Kübler-Ross encouraged participants to recall the grief they may have experienced in the past and to express those feelings. This not only enabled them to deal with loss in their lives—the loss of a friend or relative or even the loss of a marriage through divorce—but also to confront the greatest loss of all—their own death. Kübler-Ross wrote,

> There are a million little deaths as we grow, and each one could be dealt with by the expression of natural grief and tears. We would then be able to move on to new challenges in life. If loss has never been death with in an adequate healthy manner as a child, we often become bitter, depressed individuals who drown in our own self-pity and spend most of our time living in the past, regretting the "todays" and worried and fearful about the "tomorrows." Those individuals always feel misunderstood and spend most of their lives looking for others to fulfill their needs—which will never be met. We are responsible for the gratification of our own needs and our own pleasures![50]

Other emotions that can undermine an individual's life are guilt and shame. From early childhood, a person may have felt guilty about not performing well in school, not being physically attractive, or not living up to his or her parents' expectations. This can fill individuals with shame and make them feel unworthy.

From Kübler-Ross's viewpoint, love is the greatest of the human emotions. This includes the ability to express warmth and affection for another person. Another type of love is the willingness of parents to help their children achieve independence. Finally, love means unconditional acceptance of another human being, whatever their accomplishments, whatever their faults, whatever their physical disabilities.

From her work with cancer patients, Kübler-Ross realized that an individual's ability to fight a severe illness came from an inner strength. This strength was tied to the patient's state of mind. "It became very clear over these last years," she wrote, "working with healthy people as well as terminally ill patients that our only enemies are guilt, fear, and shame. Such unresolved negativities prevent us from living fully and deplete us of so much energy that even a fight with cancer is a losing battles when we have a…sense of hopelessness or a feeling of unworthiness to get well." [51]

Generally, the retreats that Kübler-Ross conducted began with people introducing themselves and explaining why they had attended. Some explained that they were going through a divorce. Others were afraid that they had contracted a terminal illness. A few had lost children to cancer or another disease. Some, in the helping professions, said they had come to learn how to be "a better nurse," "a better physician," "a better minister." As the participants talked about why they were attending the retreat, they often began sharing their feelings. At first, a dying patient might talk about feelings of anger, fear, and sadness as death approached. Other participants listened to the pain expressed by a terminally ill patient and often cried with that patient. Then, one by one, the rest of the group members were moved to talk about their own feelings. These may have involved sadness they felt over losing a child, guilt at not spending enough time with a loved one before his or her death, or anger over a recent divorce. As Kübler-Ross explained, "Sharing is the beginning. And through sharing, each patient connects with his own pain, his own [hidden] grief, his own negativities. And when this connection is made, he is given a safe place…to [express] that negativity, and get rid of it forever if he chooses to." [52]

Once the negative feelings have been expressed, Kübler-Ross believed that it was much easier for people to embrace more positive feelings. "Most people spend 90 percent of their energy and time worrying about tomorrows and live only 10 percent in the now. Once the pool of . . . negative emotions has been emptied, we can alter those percentages and live a much more full and gratifying and less draining . . . life than before."[53] As a result, individuals find much greater happiness in their lives. They are also better prepared to deal with tragedy when it strikes. One woman who participated in a workshop had to cope with the death of her son, who committed suicide a month later. In the workshop she had developed skills that helped her deal with this tragedy.

Some workshop participants helped others to deal with loss. One of the ways they did it was to establish local chapters of groups called The Compassionate Friends. This

Dougy

At her workshops, Elisabeth Kübler-Ross talked about one child, named Dougy, who had been diagnosed with a terminal illness. Dougy's parents had attended one of Kübler-Ross's lectures. Later, she met Dougy, who was battling cancer, and they talked about his illness. Sometime afterward, Kübler-Ross received a letter from Dougy. "I have only one more question left," he wrote. "What is life and what is death and why do little children have to die?" Kübler-Ross answered, "Some flowers bloom only for a few days—everybody admires and loves them as a sign of spring and hope. Then they die—but they have done what they needed to do." She added in her book *The Wheel of Life,* "There have been many thousands of people who have been helped by that letter. But it is Dougy who deserves all the credit."*

* Elisabeth Kübler-Ross, *The Wheel of Life: A Memoir of Living and Dying,* New York: Scribner, 1997, p. 227.

group was started in Coventry, England, in 1969 by Iris and Joe Lawley, and Bill and Joan Henderson. Both couples had recently lost young children and found comfort in talking about their feelings with each other. With the help of Reverend Simon Stephens, they formed a self-help group to assist other parents who had suffered a similar loss. As a chaplain of the British Royal Navy, Reverend Stephens traveled to other parts of the world and founded new chapters of Compassionate Friends. In 1972, the first chapter of Compassionate Friends in the United States was opened in Florida by Paula and Arnold Shamres. Currently there are more than 600 chapters across the United States and many others in countries around the world.

For some people, the energy to begin one of these chapters came from the Life, Death, and Transition workshop. For other participants, attending a workshop after experiencing a loss enabled them to understand and deal with it more successfully. In her book *To Live Until We Say Goodbye,* published in 1978, Kübler-Ross described one woman named Linda who had lost a child named Jamie after the little girl developed a brain tumor. Linda attended the retreat to work through her own grief and to talk about her feelings with other participants. While she was there, everyone celebrated what would have been the sixth birthday of her dead child. During the workshop, Linda met Rob, another parent who had lost a child. This had not occurred as a result of a long illness, but had happened unexpectedly when the child drowned. By listening to Linda's story, Rob was able to deal with his anger and he "became aware that he was not alone having pain." This helped him come to terms with the death of his child.[54]

For many participants, the final day of the workshop was the high point of their experience. Everyone joined together to sing songs and dance around a large fire. To symbolize the removal of their negative feelings, they "are asked to place their pain, agony, guilt, grief, fear, and shame...into a pine cone and then one after the other steps forward and throws the pine cone into the fire."[55] Thus, the workshop became a life-affirming experience, although many of the participants were coping with their own terminal illness or had recently experienced the tragedy of death in their own families.

7

The Hospice
Movement
and AIDS

One of the women who participated in Kübler-Ross's workshops was named Louise. Director of the Social Services Department in a large hospital, Louise had been diagnosed with breast cancer. As her disease grew worse, Louise was asked by the hospital to retire from her job. Louise went home, but instead of becoming depressed, she continued to reach out to patients. "Before long," Kübler-Ross wrote, "she had a truly remarkable counseling service in her living room. Terminally ill patients asked to be taken to Louise to get advice and sometimes simply to see her beaming, radiant, and truly shining face." [56]

Louise was one of those people who refused to give up, although she had a terminal illness. As Kübler-Ross put it: "In the course of a terminal illness, we can give up ... or we have the choice to complete our work, to function in whatever way we are capable and thereby touch many lives by our valiant struggle and our own sense of purpose in our own existence." [57] This was the course of action that Louise chose for herself. She spent most of her final days at home, helping other people, and living with her two large dogs—both Labrador retrievers. Kübler-Ross visited Louise during her last illness as well as other terminal patients. As Kübler-Ross said, Louise became their physician. "And I mean 'physician' in the old sense of the word: a person who is there to relieve suffering, with a clear understanding that it does not mean medical cure, medical treatment, or necessarily a prolongation of life. The patients were more concerned about the *quality* of life than the *quantity* of life. We took our cues from those patients who were willing to stop all treatment and to return home, to put their own house in order—symbolically and literally speaking—and to spend the last few weeks, months, or sometimes only days with their next of kin." [58]

Kübler-Ross's approach reflects the principles that have been embraced by the modern hospice movement. (A hospice is a program that cares for the terminally ill.) The primary role of a hospice is not to offer a cure for a terminal illness but rather to offer palliative care. This means relief from pain while also creating an environment that offers a patient the best quality of life during his or her terminal illness.

Hospice care involves a team concept that includes physicians, social workers, members of the clergy, psychologists, nurses, and volunteers. The emphasis in hospice care is on a holistic approach that treats the patient's pain as well as his or her psychological reactions to a terminal illness. According to one study, up to 50 percent of cancer patients experience pain. Indeed, pain is the major fear of patients who face a terminal illness. As a result, patients are offered painkillers whenever they need them. Patients are involved in the decision to administer painkillers as well as in all other aspects of their treatment. In addition to pain relief, patients are also offered help in coping with the emotional aspects of their illness. They may be dealing with guilt over events that occurred earlier in their life, anger because of their illness, as well as depression because their existence no longer seems to have any meaning.

In addition to treating the patient, hospice care also offers help for his or her family. Psychologists and social workers help a patient's children and spouse come to terms with the terminal illness. Volunteers help plan for the future when the terminally ill patient is no longer alive. This planning may involve care of children whose mother is dying of cancer. In addition, hospice care includes bereavement services. For months after the patient's death, hospice team members help the family grieve for their lost loved one and accept his or her death.

In many cases, hospice provides care in a patient's own home. Here the environment is usually warmer and more comfortable, away from the hi-tech machinery of a modern hospital. Often a living room becomes the place where a patient lies in bed. The living room is in the center of family life, with, as Kübler-Ross wrote,

access to the kitchen, to the smells of the soup or the coffee that was cooking, to the window which might look out onto the garden, to the spring coming up, to the trees blooming, to the mailman approaching the house, or to the children returning home from school. We wanted these patients to *live* until they died, rather than to be separated in an isolated bedroom. They had night tables with flowers that were picked by children, rather than monitors and transfusion equipment.... Any child who has experienced the death of a brother or sister, mother or father, grandfather or grandmother, in his own home, surrounded with peace and love, will not be afraid of death or dying anymore, and it is these children who will be the teachers of our next generations, of our tomorrows![59]

THE HOSPICE MOVEMENT

In England, the modern hospice movement was born. It was led by Cicely Saunders, who had been trained as a nurse and social worker and later became a doctor. Saunders worked at St. Joseph's Hospice and led the effort to provide palliative care for dying patients. In 1967, she founded St. Christopher's Hospice in London. Part of the money for the hospice was given to Dr. Saunders by a dying patient. "I went to see him," Saunders said, "and then I followed him and visited him about 25 times during the two months that he was dying in a very busy surgical ward. And he was David Tasma, and he is really the founder of the modern Hospice movement." During the 1960s, Saunders also came to the United States and taught about hospice care at Yale University School of Nursing, in Connecticut.

In 1969, the publication of Kübler-Ross's book, *On Death and Dying,* provided a further boost to the hospice movement. As *Time* magazine put it, the book "has brought death out of the darkness." The approach taken by hospice teams as they

The Hospice Tradition

Hospices are not new. They existed in the ancient world, where they served as places to treat the sick and care for the dying. Generally, they were run by religious groups, such as Hindus and Buddhists. During the Middle Ages, hospices were established on the routes to the Holy Land in the Middle East. Pilgrims traveled along these routes to visit the tomb of Jesus Christ. If pilgrims became sick along the way, they could find help at local hospices, which were run by the Christian Church. Possibly the most famous treatment center was the hospice of Saint Bernard in the Swiss Alps. There the monks who ran the hospice sent out large dogs, called St. Bernards, to rescue travelers who had been caught in the snow and bring them to safety. During the Middle Ages, many hospices were established at places where people crossed rivers or traveled through mountain passes. Since accidents might occur at these locations, hospices offered care for travelers who might suffer injuries. In England, for example, there were an estimated 750 hospices.

By the 1800s, medicine became more sophisticated. Hospitals became separated from hospices, which gradually disappeared. Hospitals were established to cure the sick, and terminally ill patients were not welcome. They were seen as medical failures—people whom medicine could not cure. During the nineteenth century, the hospice concept was revived in Ireland, which was gripped by a terrible famine that caused the deaths of hundreds of people. The first modern hospice opened in Dublin in 1870. However, the concept was slow to catch on in the West. By the middle of the twentieth century, an estimated 80 percent of people in the United States died in hospitals.

deal with the needs of dying patients is much the same as the one that Kübler-Ross has described in her lectures, workshops, and books, and in her treatment of the terminally ill. Indeed, she had long advocated that dying patients would be better served by going home rather than remaining in the hospital, although, at first, this seemed like a radical approach to helping the terminally ill.

"Very few families had considered taking their patients home to die," she wrote. "Rather it was the norm to send patients to the hospital when they were close to dying. Not only was this the norm throughout society, but it was almost expected; it implied that the family had done everything possible, that nobody was to blame, that the best specialists and the best equipment were nearby.... It was a different thought and a different philosophy when they were confronted with our opposite approach, namely: Take them to the hospital only as long as appropriate treatment is available... but take them home whenever treatment has failed to bring about positive results." [60]

In 1974, the first hospice opened in the United States. Called the Connecticut Hospice, it was followed by others in California, New York City, and Baltimore, Maryland. Many hospice programs provide care for a terminally ill patient at home. However, some hospice programs include their own facilities, where patients can live during the last part of their terminal illness. By the twenty-first century, there were more than 3,000 hospice programs in the United States. According to the most recent statistics, about 25 percent of patients who died were provided with care in a hospice program.

AIDS AND HOSPICE CARE

During the 1980s, more and more patients entering hospice care were suffering from AIDS (acquired immunodeficiency syndrome). The first AIDS cases appeared in the United States during the early 1980s. Patients were mainly homosexual men and the disease could be transmitted by sexual contact. In addition, AIDS can be developed by contact with an infected patient's blood. As a result, drug users who injected themselves with needles contracted AIDS if the needle had already been used by another person with the disease. Hospitals also began to discover that AIDS could be transmitted from a mother with the disease to a child she was carrying during her pregnancy. Consequently, babies were being born with AIDS.

During the early stages of the AIDS epidemic, very little was understood about the disease. Many people feared that they could develop AIDS by breathing the same air as an infected patient, which was untrue. National political leaders did little, at first, to deal with the AIDS problem, because it mainly afflicted homosexuals and drug users—two groups whose problems did not receive wide support among the rest of the American population.

AIDS and HIV

In patients suffering from AIDS, the immune system, which fights off diseases that enter the human body, has been fatally damaged by powerful viruses. Scientists in France and the United States discovered that HIV (human immune deficiency virus) produces AIDS. They called the viruses HIV-1 and HIV-2. These viruses enter an individual's white blood cells, which defend against disease in the body's immune system, and destroy them. As a result, AIDS patients were open to developing fatal diseases. These included a type of pneumonia, which infected their lungs. In addition, AIDS patients developed infections of their esophagus (the tube that receives food and water and transports them to the stomach), making it impossible for them to eat or drink without terrible pain. They incurred eye infections, which eventually caused blindness, and also developed Kaposi's sarcoma, a type of skin cancer that is characterized by dark tumors.

In her book, *AIDS: The Ultimate Challenge,* Kübler-Ross wrote that she received her first request in 1981 to include an AIDS patient in a Life, Death, and Transition workshop. At this time, AIDS patients received very little help or understanding from the rest of the community. Most people were afraid to be near them, but Kübler-Ross did not hesitate. "Naturally," she said. "We have never ever discriminated, and all terminally ill patients have always been welcome."[61] The AIDS patient, named Bob, described to the other workshop participants his sad, frustrating battle with the disease.

At first, he couldn't believe that any disease like AIDS could strike down a young man who was only 27 years old. "He went from shock to denial," Kübler-Ross explained, "from anger and rage to bargaining with God. There were days when he was so depressed he could neither eat nor sleep. The sores in his mouth and throat added to his discomfort.... He avoided his family out of fear of their reaction and started to isolate himself totally."[62] Finally, Bob said, he told his mother about his illness in a long tearful telephone call. The reaction among the other participants at the workshop was overwhelmingly supportive. When Bob had finished his story, Kübler-Ross recalled, the others gathered around him and sang, "I'll be loving you, always."

WORKSHOPS FOR AIDS PATIENTS

Soon afterward, Kübler-Ross began running workshops exclusively for AIDS patients. Their numbers were rapidly growing and the demand for her services was increasing. Many of the participants described the physical pain of the disease as well as the psychological pain they endured in their community. AIDS patients were often shunned by the rest of the population who were fearful of catching the disease from them. As the patients grew weaker, some relied on a close friend to care for them. Others turned to their mothers, who came to live with them. Some of these women attended Kübler-Ross's seminars.

As she wrote in her book, these caregivers were middle-aged and older. Each woman had already raised her children, then, suddenly, she was thrust back into that same role once again. Their sons were too weak to care for themselves, and these women had to nurse them through their final illness. Kübler-Ross visited some of these patients during her lecture tours around the United States. She recalled one woman, who took her to the apartment she shared with her dying son. "I gave him a butterfly, the symbol of our transition (from earth), and explained to him that we only leave the physical body—the soul leaves and we will be whole again after what we call death. He wanted to know all about the light we encounter...."[63]

WOMEN AND CHILDREN WITH AIDS

In addition to adults who developed AIDS, children also contracted the disease. Some inherited it from their mothers while growing in their wombs. Others received a blood transfusion (transfer of blood from one person to another), after they were born, from donors who had been infected with AIDS. In 1985, during a speech at Mary Baldwin College in Staunton, Virginia, Kübler-Ross announced that she was planning to open a hospice for AIDS babies. She wanted to build the hospice at Healing Waters Farm. This was her new home in Virginia, where she had moved a year earlier from California.

Unfortunately, Kübler-Ross's announcement was greeted with strong opposition from many of the people who lived around her. As one of them wrote in a letter to the editor of the local newspaper: "Why should we bring a disease such as this to our county? Many residents know little or nothing about this disease." After praising political leaders for bringing more jobs into the area, the writer added, "Why not bring something else... to create more jobs instead of an AIDS center. How many people do you expect to work around such a contagious disease? I won't."[64]

Another writer pointed out: "Have you stopped to consider what effect this center will have on our county? The taxes will go up drastically as soon as they begin operation, especially if there are any school-aged children. They will demand educational classes and the county will have to comply. The land values will go down, as people who were expecting to come to our county to live will go elsewhere. And any chance of economic growth will go out the window."[65]

At a county-wide meeting to consider the hospice, Kübler-Ross was booed when she entered the room. No one wanted to listen to her reasons for establishing the hospice; they simply wanted her to leave the area. After the meeting was over, her windows were shot out at night, and sharp objects were placed in her driveway to give her truck flat tires. As a result of the opposition to the hospice, Kübler-Ross knew she could not receive a permit from the community to build it. Therefore, she eventually gave up her idea. Nevertheless, she continued working with AIDS babies, trying to find families who would adopt the infants and care for them.

She also counseled adults who had developed the disease, not only men but a growing number of women as well. Many of them felt isolated from the rest of society, which did not seem to care about them. One of these patients, named Bonny, attended a Life, Death, and Transition workshop. Friends and co-workers had abandoned her. At the beginning of the seminar, participants stand up to introduce themselves. Bonny stood up and said: "I am here because I am dying of AIDS." Bonny was afraid that others in the workshop would start to leave, afraid to be around her. "Without another word spoken," Dr. Kübler-Ross wrote,

> one of the cancer patients got up from her wheelchair. [Bonny] was convinced that she would be the first one to leave the workshop. Who would want to share a week in such close proximity with someone who had AIDS? But

the cancer patient did not head toward the door. With a staggering, unsure gait, she headed straight toward Bonny. She kneeled down to her and hugged her; the tears intermingled and she found a friend! [66]

After the seminar ended, Bonny's new friends continued to visit her throughout the last phase of her illness.

As Kübler-Ross explained, the workshops provided a training ground for many people who later became volunteers, helping AIDS patients. Others who attended workshops later directed programs for AIDS victims. Gradually, scientists increased their understanding of the disease and developed more effective methods of fighting it. Communities also increased their empathy for those who had contracted AIDS and established many new programs to help these patients.

Helping the Dying and Their Families

8

Elisabeth Kübler-Ross continued her work in the field of thanatology during the 1980s and early 1990s. She lectured in the United States, Europe, and Africa, and ran weeklong workshops from her home at Healing Waters. She also counseled individual patients suffering from terminal illness, as well as their families.

Much of her counseling focused on the needs of children. In her book *Living With Death and Dying*, Kübler-Ross described the problems of a third-grade girl who seemed lost in her own sadness and refused to communicate with the other children at her school. Finally, her teacher called Kübler-Ross to ask if she might see the little girl and her younger sister. Meanwhile, Kübler-Ross had learned that the girls' mother was dying of cancer and their father refused to talk about the illness with his children. Although young children might not directly talk about a dying parent, Kübler-Ross had earlier realized that they often expressed their feelings through drawings. No one may have told them that a parent was dying, but the children always seemed to know what was happening.

COMMUNICATING FEELINGS THROUGH DRAWINGS

She invited the little girls to her house on a cold December day. While seated at the kitchen table, the third grader drew a picture of a stick figure with very large red legs. Kübler-Ross asked the little girl about the person in the picture. The girl answered that it was her mother and that her legs "are very sick," and she would never again be able to take her walking in the park. Next to her mother, the girl had drawn a table that had been overturned. When Kübler-Ross asked her about the table, the girl answered: "Yes, you see my mommy will also never again eat with us at the dinner table." Kübler-Ross picked up the fact that the girl kept repeating the word "never." She asked whether her mother was going to die. And the girl answered that this would occur shortly—indeed, her mother was in a coma—and that she would then go to heaven. "I asked her to imagine a cocoon that really looked as if there was no life inside," Kübler-Ross wrote,

> We pictured a cocoon together, and I was just explaining that at the right time, every cocoon opens up and out of it comes…when she hollered, 'A butterfly.' We talked for a while about how death was not the end…. [Butterflies] fly away and we do not see them, but they then only begin to enjoy the flowers and the sunshine. Both children sat with open eyes, quite delighted about this possibility.

Afterward, they were taken to the hospital. Although their mother was in a coma, they said to her 'Mommy, soon you are going to be as free as a butterfly.' They saw their father in the hospital room, and together, as a family, shared their reactions about death. Afterward, the little girl discussed her experience in school and her classmates added their own recollections about deaths that had occurred in their families.[67]

Kübler-Ross recognized that death was often a taboo subject, and most people were afraid to discuss it, unless they received some kind of prompting. Adults were afraid to discuss the subject with children, and children often hesitated to address the subject directly. They knew about death and talked about it symbolically, however—through pictures and by acting out their feelings. One patient whom Kübler-Ross saw was a 13-year-old boy, confined to a hospital where he faced possible death unless he received a kidney transplant. Among the other patients were ill and dying children. Each day the boy would walk around the corridors and pretend to shoot some of the little girls who were lying in the rooms. The staff was mystified at his actions and annoyed by his behavior. They asked Kübler-Ross to talk to him. She discussed the boy's behavior with him and asked why he only shot some of the patients. "Did you notice I not only pick little girls, but they all have good kidneys?" he answered. He seemed to know which patients were not suffering from kidney problems, and who could help him with a healthy kidney before it was too late.[68] This was the boy's symbolic way of expressing his own fears about death and trying to do something about obtaining a new kidney to save himself.

KNOWING THAT DEATH IS IMMINENT

In her writings, Kübler-Ross often stated that terminally ill patients seemed to know intuitively when their death was at

Susan

A child named Susan was terminally ill with a lung disease. She lived inside an oxygen tent in the hospital; the oxygen kept her alive. However, the child seemed to sense that death was approaching. Although she did not speak about it directly, she asked her nurse one night what would happen if a fire started while she was in the tent. At first, the nurse tried to reassure her that such a disaster could never happen. Only later, after talking to her supervisor, did the nurse realize that the little girl really wanted to discuss something else. Both nurses visited with the girl and asked her about her fear of the fire. Then, the supervisor lay down in the bed beside her. "The child started to cry," Kübler-Ross wrote. "She thought for a while and then said in plain English, 'I know I'm going to die very soon and just have to talk to somebody about it.' " Unfortunately, the nurses were the only ones to whom the child could speak. Although the child wanted to talk to her mother, her mother could not deal with the child's coming death and would not talk to her about it. As a result, mother and child were unable to say all the things that they might have said before the girl died. The child died soon afterward, without ever fulfilling her wish to talk to her mother about death.*

* Elisabeth Kübler-Ross, *Living With Death and Dying: How to Communicate With the Terminally Ill*, New York: Simon and Schuster, 1997, p. 21.

hand. As she made her rounds in the hospitals to visit dying patients, Kübler-Ross explained that she often shook hands with them. "A dying patient holds my hand differently, and I look at her and say, 'Is this the last time?' The patient then nods her head. I then say good-bye to her and the next morning the bed is empty."[69] One elderly patient in the hospital gave Kübler-Ross his cane as a gift when she visited him. She was about to tell him that he might need it, but she stopped herself and said nothing. Shortly afterward, he died.

In her book *Death Is of Vital Importance,* Kübler-Ross told the story of a woman who had gone to visit her elderly grandmother. The old woman took a ring from her finger and put it on the finger of her granddaughter. "'You really want *me* to have it?' [Grandma nodded.] And then the granddaughter said, 'Why don't you ...' and then she stopped what she intended to say, which was, 'Why don't you wait and give it to me for Christmas,' because she immediately knew that Grandma must know that she would not be here at Christmas any more." Indeed, Grandma died before Christmas arrived.[70]

This elderly woman had reached the stage of acceptance, which Kübler-Ross had described many years earlier in her explanation of the various phases that dying patients experience as they deal with terminal illness. Unfortunately, many patients may never reach that stage. Kübler-Ross described a 21-year-old man who was dying from cancer. He had been in the hospital for six weeks but refused to speak to any member of the staff who visited him. When Kübler-Ross went to see him, he treated her the same way. From his bed, he simply stared at a wall that was covered with get-well cards from his family and friends. Kübler-Ross was about to leave, but finally she said to him: "'Bob, doesn't that make you mad? You lie on your back in this room for six weeks staring at this wall covered with pink, green, and blue get-well cards?' He turned around abruptly, pouring out his rage, anger, and envy, directly at all the people who could be outside enjoying the sunshine, going shopping, picking a fancy get-well-soon card, when they knew darn well he wasn't going to get well."[71]

The families of dying patients react in much the same as the terminally ill, themselves. Kübler-Ross took one woman to her office, so she could yell with rage because her child was dying in the hospital. Some pass through the stage of anger and rage, then experience sadness and depression over the death of a loved one. One woman expressed her sadness over her dying child, Jeffy, in a poem, titled "Hospital Playroom":

> Come to the playroom and look inside
> See all the toys of the children who have died.
> There is Beth Ann's doll and a book from Mary
> A bat and a ball and a mitt from Larry....
>
> I wonder what of Jeffy's we'll give
> To this graveyard that said these children lived.
> A puzzle, a book, or his shiny new bike?
> His fire engine or the red old trike?
>
> It's supposed to be fun to come here and play
> With a sick little child made happy today.
> But my eyes and my heart from this place want to go
> It's filled with the ghosts of the children we know.[72]

EXPERIENCING HER PERSONAL LOSSES

As Elisabeth Kübler-Ross helped families deal with the loss represented by death, she was dealing with different kinds of loss in her own life. In 1988, while lecturing in Europe, she stopped to visit one of her sisters in Switzerland. The next morning, as Kübler-Ross came downstairs for breakfast, she suddenly experienced a massive weakness inside her body. She was convinced that she was dying. Instead of starting to panic, however, she decided that she had been given an opportunity to describe her own death in the few minutes remaining to her. Remarkably, she focused on her own experience of dying and how it might contribute to others who wanted to understand how their death might feel.

She wasn't afraid, Kübler-Ross told her sister. Suddenly, she said that she had left her own body. Then she explained that she was heading toward a bright light. "'Here I come!' I screamed."[73] Kübler-Ross did not die at her sister's home. What she had experienced was a slight heart problem. She returned to her farm at Healing Waters, and a short time later took off for Europe again. After coming back to Virginia, she experienced a stroke that left her right side temporarily paralyzed. Kübler-Ross was taken to the hospital and treated, then brought home to heal. After a week in bed, she began walking around with the help of a cane and hiking across the hills on her farm at Healing Waters.

Two years later, in 1990, Kübler-Ross opened the Elisabeth Kübler-Ross Center at Healing Waters for her Life, Death, and Transition workshops. She also continued running programs for those who could not come to Healing Waters. In 1991, she held her first workshop in a prison to help inmates. At a prison in Scotland, inmates described their crimes and shared their feelings with each other. In 1992, Kübler-Ross journeyed to South Africa, where she held a workshop in Johannesburg.

Meanwhile, Kübler-Ross had been told that her ex-husband, Manny Ross, was seriously ill. He had heart surgery in Chicago, and afterwards moved to Arizona, where the climate was warmer. Kübler-Ross visited him there, but their time together was brief. Once he reached Arizona, Manny continued to experience severe health problems, and died.

In 1994, Kübler-Ross experienced another loss, when her home at Healing Waters was destroyed by fire. She suspected that the fire had been set by someone in the area who was still angry at her over the proposal to build an AIDS hospice for babies. Although Kübler-Ross planned to stay in Virginia and build a new center, her son Kenneth convinced her to move to Phoenix, where he lived.

In 1995, Kübler-Ross experienced a series of strokes, which paralyzed much of her left side. She was admitted to the hospital and afterward was brought home to recover. This time, however, she did not make the type of recovery that occurred after her previous stroke. Instead, she has remained dependent on caregivers to provide her with support so she can continue to live. She no longer lectures, sees patients, or runs her workshops. As Kübler-Ross put it: "I am like a plane that has left the gate and not taken off. I would rather go back to the gate or fly away." [74]

After her stroke, Kübler-Ross continued to improve. On her website, she reported in 2000 that "I am still feeding about 200 birds outside my living room window and 14 coyotes.... My garden is neglected, since I cannot walk anymore." In 2002, she visited New York City with her son Kenneth, where she met many people who had participated in her workshops. Later that year, she traveled with her family to Switzerland to attend the funeral of her sister Erika. Unfortunately, on her return home, Kübler-Ross suffered a bad fall and had to be admitted to a group home.

Dr. Kübler-Ross's Legacy

9

During the twentieth century, Elisabeth Kübler-Ross led the effort to raise the level of awareness among those in the medical establishment as well as the general population about the needs of the dying. She also provided a spark to the development of the modern hospice movement that provides care for the terminally ill. For many years before Kübler-Ross's work, medicine had focused on curing patients, not dealing with the problems of the terminally ill. With its reliance on high-tech instruments and modern methods of research, medicine had succeeded in saving more and more patients who might have died in the past. Doctors often equated success with curing a sick patient, not with losing a patient to terminal illness.

Elisabeth Kübler-Ross changed the focus of medicine. Her struggle was not an easy one. She continually encountered a medical community that did not agree with her. Physicians denied Kübler-Ross the right to interview terminally ill patients. Kübler-Ross would not give up, however. As a young person she had proved that she was not afraid to defy authority. Her father did not want her to become a doctor, but she refused to listen, attended medical school in Switzerland, and eventually became a successful psychiatrist.

As a psychiatrist, she knew how to listen to patients. Kübler-Ross used her skills to listen to dying patients and empathize with their plight. She learned from them how they felt about facing death. She also talked to their families and discovered what they were experiencing as they coped with the death of a loved one. In 1969, she published a groundbreaking book based on her work with the terminally ill, *On Death and Dying.* The book became an international best-seller and was widely used in programs taught in universities that focused on working with the terminally ill.

In her book, Kübler-Ross described five stages that terminally ill patients pass through as they approach death. The first stage is the initial shock that a person feels on learning that he or she has a terminal illness. At first, the patient tries to deny that the illness exists. In the next stage, a patient may become angry because he or she is dying. The patient may also feel jealous of other people who have not been stricken with a terminal disease. In the third stage, some patients bargain with God or with their doctor to give them more time to live. One woman, for example, asked to stay alive until her child finished school. During the next stage, patients often experience depression and grief, as they recognize that their death may occur shortly. Finally, some patients reach the stage of acceptance, where they face their death peacefully.

Kübler-Ross did not believe that these stages necessarily occurred one after the other. Patients, she said, may move back and forth among several stages simultaneously. Some patients never reach acceptance, and a few remain stuck in the denial phase. Kübler-Ross believed that by listening and talking to patients, however, caregivers such as nurses, social workers, doctors, and members of the clergy could help them accept their death. Communication also helped the families of dying patients, who may have been going through the same stages as the patients themselves.

Many family members react to the news that a loved one is dying with shock, denial, and anger. They are often unwilling to talk to a terminally ill loved one about his or her coming death. As a result, both the patient and the family remain isolated, unable to complete what Kübler-Ross described as their "unfinished business." They can talk about mistakes they might have made in their relationships and try to set things "right" before death occurs.

Following the publication of *On Death and Dying,* Kübler-Ross began giving lectures across the world to terminally ill patients as well as to a variety of caregivers. She opened a center in California where she conducted weeklong workshops on death and dying. In addition, Kübler-Ross continued to counsel dying patients and their families who needed her help.

CHALLENGES TO THE WORK OF KÜBLER-ROSS

Although Elisabeth Kübler-Ross's ideas revolutionized the entire field of thanatology, some experts have questioned her work. Michele Catherine Gantois Chaban, a social worker who counsels the dying, did extensive research on the life of Kübler-Ross. In her book, *The Life Work of Dr. Elisabeth Kübler-Ross and Its Impact on the Death Awareness Movement*, Chaban points out that Kübler-Ross never documented her work with dying patients that led to the publication of her revolutionary book in 1969. Although Kübler-Ross said that she interviewed more than 200 terminally ill patients, she did not explain much about them. Most scientific researchers generally would have included information describing such things as the age and gender of the patients, whether or not they knew that they were dying, and whether the patient's family was included in the interviews. None of this information was provided in Kübler-Ross's book.

Ms. Chaban also questioned whether Kübler-Ross actually began and led the seminars at the University of Chicago that involved dying patients. During the program, she worked with the Reverend Carl Nighswonger, Director of Pastoral [Religious] Care at the University of Chicago hospital. Nighswonger claimed that he had started the program on death and dying. He said that Kübler-Ross joined it later as his assistant. Nighswonger also explained that he had developed various stages that dying patients pass through as they approach death. They experienced *denial, depression, bargaining, despair,* and *acceptance.*

Nighswonger further claimed that his work was based on the research of another scientist who had also developed a stage theory to describe the experiences of the terminally ill. These stages included, "false hope," when the patient receives treatment for the disease, which may even seem to disappear for a while. When the terminal illness returns, however, the patient falls into "despair." As a result, a patient may become angry and feel bitter toward God for allowing such a thing to happen. Some patients eventually reach a stage of accepting their fate, which includes a feeling of peace.[75]

According to a student of Nighswonger and Kübler-Ross, both scientists worked on the death and dying project together. Indeed, after interviews with patients, they would sit together and decide into which stage of dying the patient seemed to fall. However, Chaplain Herman Cook, who also assisted Kübler-Ross, stated that she was the person who initiated the seminars and took the lead in developing the new theories of death and dying. As he put it in a letter to Chaban: "Elisabeth was the dominant figure and authority in the seminar.... Furthermore, her professional status had more clout than that of a chaplain. That, and her book, catapulted her into worldwide fame. She had more charisma than Carl...and more intelligence."[76] (For more information on Reverend Nighswonger, please enter "Carl Nighswonger" into any search engine and browse the sites listed.)

As Kübler-Ross herself explained, "My work with 'the stages of dying,' long preceded my meeting with these two chaplains [Nighswonger and Cook], as I learned the stages from parents of multiple-handicapped, retarded, and blind children, who went through the same stages in coming to grips with the awareness of a blind infant or a multiple-handicapped baby, but since no one asked me to write a book about it, it only came into print when I was asked...to write about the stages of dying. It is totally insignificant to me who gets credit for this. My sole purpose is to share with people that patients in crisis, in anger, and in grief have to be allowed to externalize [talk] and accept those feelings without critics' judgment."[77]

Before working with dying patients in Chicago during the 1960s, Kübler-Ross counseled blind and handicapped children and their parents. The sense of loss that these parents experienced was similar to the sense of loss that dying patients and their families feel. They often pass through the same stages.

In the early years of her work in the field of thanatology, Elisabeth Kübler-Ross did not have a belief in life after death. As she put it: "I have worked with dying patients for the last 20 years. When I started this work, I must say, I was neither very interested in life after death nor did I have any really clear picture about the definition of death. When you study the scientific definition of death, you see that it only includes the death of a physical body, as if man would only exist as the cocoon. I was one of the physicians and scientists who did not ever question that."[78]

From this cocoon, Kübler-Ross eventually became convinced that human beings emerge and become like butterflies. They

Stages of Loss

The stages that Kübler-Ross theorized that dying patients go through have also been applied to other types of loss. These include the loss of a job or the loss of a marriage through divorce. The initial reaction may be shock or disbelief. "I can't be losing my job," or "You can't be serious about wanting a divorce." This stage is often followed by anger, "Why is this happening to me and not to someone else?" A few people remain locked in the stage of anger for years. In cases of divorce, for example, husbands and wives may be extremely angry with each other over issues such as custody of their children and division of their property—houses, cars, furniture, and so on. Some people try to bargain. They might ask to be kept in their job, for example, until they can find another one. Or a woman may ask her husband to stay in the marriage and give it one more chance. If he refuses, a sense of despair or depression sets in over the loss of what had existed in the past. Individuals may also feel depressed because of the need to make difficult changes. Most people, however, eventually work through the despair to a state of acceptance and continue with their lives.

pass into a spiritual world after their deaths. Kübler-Ross had seen butterflies drawn on the walls by children who were killed at the Nazi concentration camp of Maidanek, Poland. During the 1970s, her belief in an afterlife grew much stronger when she had her first out-of-body experience.

Kübler-Ross had gone to sleep after being exhausted from giving a workshop:

> I ... drifted off into a deep, trance-like sleep. ... I saw myself lifted out of my physical body. ... it was as if a whole lot of loving beings were taking all the tired parts out of me, similar to car mechanics in a car repair shop. It was as if they were replacing every tired and worn-out part of my physical body with a new, fresh, energized part. I experienced a great sense of peace and serenity, a feeling of literally being taken care of, of having no worry in the world.[79]

Afterward, she woke up completely refreshed and no longer feeling tired.

Kübler-Ross also described dying patients who had talked of near-death experiences. Indeed, she later claimed to have interviewed 25,000 people who described these experiences, although no data on the interviews was ever published. From these interviews, Kübler-Ross discussed some of the elements that all of these patients described. They experienced "a rush of air or wind," then saw the emergency medical teams trying to save them. In other words, they seemed to become separated from their bodies, and looked down as the rescue squads did their work. Meanwhile, a spiritual self had gone to another existence. The spiritual self was led by friends and family members who had died in the past. Eventually, because their bodies were revived, the patients returned from this other existence to resume their lives on earth.

According to Kübler-Ross, out-of-body and near-death experiences were clear evidence that there was no death, but that after our bodies died, our spirits continued to live in another world. She even described various experiences that the spirits encounter.

Clearly, this belief helped Kübler-Ross to reassure dying patients that their existence would not end with death. Like the butterfly, they would emerge from a cocoon—their bodies— and fly off somewhere else. Most scientists, however, disagreed with Kübler-Ross's views. They do not believe that she has proven with hard evidence that there is no death. Indeed, some medical experts have even said that she has undermined all of her work in thanatology by making such statements about life after death.

Today, Kübler-Ross remains a controversial pioneer in the field of medicine. Although she has made enormous contributions to the study of death and dying, some of her views and opinions continue to be hotly disputed.

1926 Elisabeth Kübler is born in Zurich, Switzerland

1939 World War II begins in Europe

1944 Goes to work in laboratory in Canton Hospital, Zurich

1945 Volunteers to work in France with the International Voluntary Service for Peace

Timeline

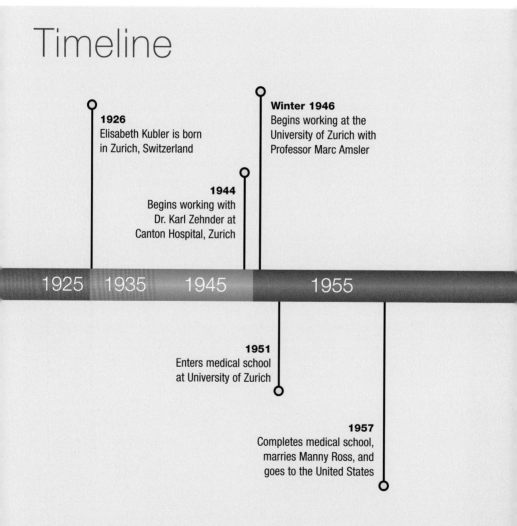

1926
Elisabeth Kubler is born
in Zurich, Switzerland

Winter 1946
Begins working at the
University of Zurich with
Professor Marc Amsler

1944
Begins working with
Dr. Karl Zehnder at
Canton Hospital, Zurich

1925 1935 1945 1955

1951
Enters medical school
at University of Zurich

1957
Completes medical school,
marries Manny Ross, and
goes to the United States

1946 Secures a position at the University of Zurich

1947 Travels to Warsaw to do volunteer work

1951 Enters medical school

1957 Completes medical school and marries
Emmanuel Ross; the couple travels to the
United States

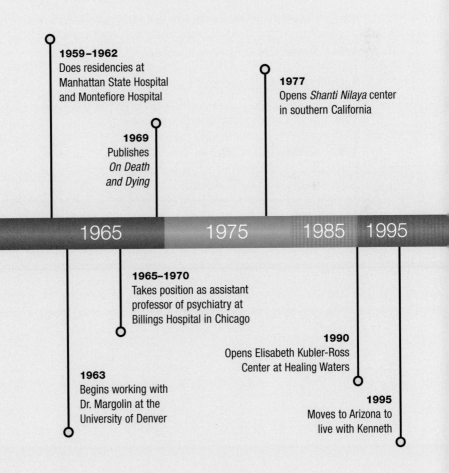

1959–1962
Does residencies at
Manhattan State Hospital
and Montefiore Hospital

1977
Opens *Shanti Nilaya* center
in southern California

1969
Publishes
*On Death
and Dying*

1965 1975 1985 1995

1965–1970
Takes position as assistant
professor of psychiatry at
Billings Hospital in Chicago

1990
Opens Elisabeth Kubler-Ross
Center at Healing Waters

1963
Begins working with
Dr. Margolin at the
University of Denver

1995
Moves to Arizona to
live with Kenneth

Chronology

1958–1959   Does an internship at Community Hospital, Glen Cove, Long Island

1959–1962   Residencies at Manhattan State Hospital and Montefiore Hospital

1962–1965   Teaches and works at University of Colorado Medical School

1965–1970   Was made assistant professor of psychiatry, Billings Hospital, University of Chicago

1969   Publishes *On Death and Dying*

1977   Opens Shanti Nilaya Growth and Healing Center

1984   Moves to Healing Waters, Virginia

1990   Opens Elisabeth Kübler-Ross Center

1991   Begins first workshop with prison inmates

1992   Lectures in South Africa

1995   Moves to Arizona; suffers strokes

Notes

Chapter 1

1. Elisabeth Kübler-Ross, *Questions and Answers on Death and Dying.* New York: Macmillan, 1974, p. 22.

2. Elisabeth Kübler-Ross, *Living with Death and Dying: How to Communicate With the Terminally Ill.* New York: Simon & Schuster, 1981, p. 57.

Chapter 2

3. Elisabeth Kübler-Ross, *The Wheel of Life: A Memoir of Living and Dying.* New York: Scribner, 1997, p. 25.

4. Ibid., p. 28.

5. Ibid., p. 29.

6. Derek Gill. *Quest: The Life of Elisabeth Kübler-Ross.* New York: Harper and Row, 1980, p. 47.

7. Ibid., p. 54.

8. Ibid., p. 79.

9. Ibid., p. 111.

10. Ibid., p. 116.

11. *The Wheel of Life,* p. 72.

12. *Quest,* p. 154.

13. *The Wheel of Life,* p. 102.

Chapter 3

14. *Quest,* p. 195.

15. Ibid., p. 201.

16. Ibid., p. 216.

17. *The Wheel of Life,* p. 123.

18. Ibid., p. 127.

19. *Quest,* p. 239.

20. Ibid., p. 246.

21. *The Wheel of Life,* p. 133.

Chapter 4

22. Elisabeth Kübler-Ross, *On Death and Dying.* New York: Scribner, 1997, p. 37.

23. *Quest,* p. 285.

24. *On Death and Dying,* p. 44.

25. Ibid., p. 49.

26. *On Death and Dying,* p. 51.

27. Ibid., p. 52.

28. Ibid., p. 63.

29. Ibid., p. 65.

30. Ibid., p. 99.

31. Ibid., p. 124.

32. Ibid., p. 149.

Chapter 5

33. *Quest,* p. 308.

34. Elisabeth Kübler-Ross, *On Children and Death.* New York: Macmillan, 1983, p. 82.

35. *The Wheel of Life,* p. 181.

36. *On Children and Death,* p. 189.

37. Ibid., p. 2.

38. Ibid., p. 190.

39. Ibid., p. 46.

40. Elisabeth Kübler-Ross, *Questions and Answers on Death and Dying.* New York: Macmillan, 1974, p. 10.

41. Ibid., p. 37.

42. Ibid., p. 61.

43. *On Children and Death,* pp. 7–8.

44. *Questions and Answers,* p. 88.

Notes

Chapter 6

45. Kay Bartlett, "No Stranger to Death, Kübler-Ross Turns Her Attention to Aids," *The Los Angeles Times*, May 10, 1987.

46. Ibid.

47. *The Wheel of Life*, p. 192.

48. Elisabeth Kübler-Ross, *Working It Through*, New York: Macmillan, 1982, p. 24.

49. Ibid., p. 34.

50. Ibid., p. 35.

51. Ibid., p. 42.

52. Ibid., pp. 44–45.

53. *Working It Through*, p. 46.

54. Ibid., p. 73.

55. Ibid., p. 61.

Chapter 7

56. Elisabeth Kübler-Ross, *To Live Until We Say Good-Bye*. Englewood Cliffs: Prentice-Hall, 1978, p. 85.

57. Ibid., p. 14.

58. Ibid., p. 21.

59. Ibid., pp. 22–23.

60. Ibid., pp. 129–130.

61. Elisabeth Kübler-Ross, *AIDS: The Ultimate Challenge*. New York: Macmillan, 1987, p. 15.

62. Ibid., p. 17.

63. Ibid., p. 34.

64. Ibid., p. 108.

65. Ibid., p. 116.

66. Ibid., pp. 152–153.

67. Elisabeth Kübler-Ross, *Living With Death and Dying: How to Communicate With the Terminally Ill*, New York: Simon & Schuster, 1997, pp. 13–16.

Chapter 8

68. Ibid., pp. 19–20.

69. Ibid., p. 23.

70. Elisabeth Kübler-Ross, *Death Is of Vital Importance: On Life, Death, and Life After Death*. Barrytown, NY: Station Hill Press, 1995, p. 7.

71. *Living With Death and Dying*, pp. 36–37.

72. Ibid., pp. 56–57.

73. *The Wheel of Life*, pp. 258–259.

74. *http://www.elisabethkublerross.com*.

75. Michele Catherine Gantois Chaban, *The Life Work of Dr. Elisabeth Kübler-Ross and Its Impact on the Death Awareness Movement*. Wales, England: The Edwin Mellen Press, 2000, p. 216.

76. Ibid., p. 165.

77. Ibid., p. 222.

78. Ibid., p. 235.

79. *Working It Through*, p. 23.

Gill, Derek. *Quest: The Life of Elisabeth Kübler-Ross.* New York: Harper and Row, 1980.

Kübler-Ross, Elisabeth. *Death, The Final Stage of Growth.* Englewood Cliffs, NJ: Prentice-Hall, 1975.

Kübler-Ross, Elisabeth. *Living With Death and Dying: How to Communicate With the Terminally Ill.* New York: Simon & Schuster, 1981.

Kübler-Ross, Elisabeth. *On Children and Death.* New York: Macmillan, 1983.

Kübler-Ross, Elisabeth. *On Death and Dying.* New York: Scribner, 1997.

Kübler-Ross, Elisabeth. *The Wheel of Life.* New York: Scribner, 1997.

Kübler-Ross, Elisabeth. *Working It Through.* New York: Macmillan, 1982.

Further Reading

Canfield, Jack. *Chicken Soup for the Kid's Soul.* New York: Scholastic, 1999.

Rofes, Eric, ed. *The Kids' Book About Death and Dying.* Boston: Little Brown, 1995.

Sanders, Pete, and Steve Myers. *Death and Dying.* New York: Copper Beach Books, 1998.

Stein, Sara. *About Dying: An Open Family Book for Parents and Children Together.* New York: Walker, 1974.

Worth, Richard. *You'll Be Old Someday, Too.* New York: Franklin Watts, 1986.

Index

Index

Index

Index

page:

26: Copyright Ken Ross	34: Copyright Ken Ross
27: Copyright Ken Ross	35: Copyright Ken Ross
28: Copyright Ken Ross	36: Copyright Ken Ross
29: Copyright Ken Ross	37: © Bettmann/CORBIS
30: Copyright Ken Ross	38: © Leonard McCombe/TimeLife
31: Copyright Ken Ross	Pictures/Getty Images
32: Copyright Ken Ross	39: Copyright Ken Ross
33: Copyright Ken Ross	

Cover: Copyright Ken Ross

About the Author

Richard Worth has thirty years of experience as a writer, trainer, and video producer. He has written more than 25 books, including *The Four Levers of Corporate Change*, a best-selling business book. Many of his books are for young adults on topics that include family living, foreign affairs, biography, history, and the criminal justice system.

LOS ALAMOS COUNTY LIBRARY
Mesa Public Library
2400 Central Avenue
Los Alamos, NM 87544-4014